A-LEVEL

STUD

EDEXCEL

Politics

Government and politics of the USA and comparative politics

Andrew Colclough and Sarra Jenkins

Series editor: Eric Magee

HODDER
EDUCATION
AN HACHETTE UK COMPANY

Hodder Education, an Hachette UK company, Blenheim Court, George Street, Banbury, Oxfordshire OX16 5BH

Orders

Bookpoint Ltd, 130 Park Drive, Milton Park, Abingdon, Oxfordshire OX14 4SB

tel: 01235 827720

fax: 01235 400401

e-mail: education@bookpoint.co.uk

Lines are open 9.00 a.m.–5.00 p.m., Monday to Saturday, with a 24-hour message answering service. You can also order through the Hodder Education website: www.hoddereducation.co.uk

© Andrew Colclough and Sarra Jenkins 2017

ISBN 978-1-4718-9293-6

First printed 2017

Impression number 5 4 3 2 1

Year 2021 2020 2019 2018 2017

This Guide has been written specifically to support students preparing for the Edexcel A-level Politics examination. The content has been neither approved nor endorsed by Edexcel and remains the sole responsibility of the author.

Typeset by Integra Software Services Pvt. Ltd., Pondicherry, India

Printed in Slovenia

Hachette UK's policy is to use papers that are natural, renewable and recyclable products and made from wood grown in sustainable forests. The logging and manufacturing processes are expected to conform to the environmental regulations of the country of origin.

Contents

■ Getting the most from this book

Exam tips

Advice on key points in the text to help you learn and recall content, avoid pitfalls, and polish your exam technique in order to boost your grade.

Knowledge check

Rapid-fire questions throughout the Content Guidance section to check your understanding.

Knowledge check answers

1 Turn to the back of the book for the Knowledge check answers.

Summaries

■ Each core topic is rounded off by a bullet-list summary for quick-check reference of what you need to know.

Exam-style questions

Questions & Answers

■ Section C questions

Note: Section C questions will be asked on *entirely* United States topics.

Question 1

Evaluate the significance of midterm elections. [30 marks]

The significance of midterms can be evaluated by looking at how specific midterm elections change the way in which politics operates, such as the impact on the power of the president or the effectiveness of Congress. This question focuses specifically on midterms (those elections in the middle of a president's term) and not elections for president or congressional elections which take place at the same time as the presidential election.

Commentary on the questions

Tips on what you need to do to gain full marks, indicated by the icon **e**

Student answer

Midterm elections are significant because they offer citizens an opportunity to vote for Congress in the middle of a president's term in office. This adds democratic value to the US voting system with elections being held at frequent intervals. In addition, the significance of midterms can be judged by their impact. Midterm elections can have a major bearing on the power of political parties (through control of Congress), the power of the incumbent president and the policy direction of the country. On the other hand their significance may not be particularly high when they lead to little or no change in these areas. Some midterms may simply maintain the status quo.

This is a good introduction for a 30-mark essay. It demonstrates a focus on the topic (of midterms) and a clear understanding of the key word 'significance', showing how the answer will evaluate that significance, by examining the impact of midterms in different ways. This also serves to give an outline of the key points covered in the answer.

Midterms are highly significant because they can lead to a major decline in presidential power. This occurs when the president's party goes from majority to minority control in one or more chambers. This leaves the president facing a hostile majority which is more likely to scrutinise presidential actions and oppose his policies. President Obama faced a major loss of power in the 2010 midterms when the Democrats lost control of the House. Congressional Republicans then opposed his policies as well as using committees to investigate the executive branch. Midterms are highly significant because they can lead to a major decline in presidential power. This occurs when the president's party goes from majority to minority control in one or more chambers. This leaves the president facing a hostile majority which is more likely to scrutinise presidential actions and oppose his policies. President Obama faced a major loss of power in the 2010 midterms when the Democrats lost control of the House. Congressional Republicans then opposed his policies as well as using committees to investigate the executive branch. Having achieved legislative success with the Affordable

Commentary on the questions

Tips on what you need to do to gain full marks, indicated by the icon **e**

Sample student answers

Practise the questions, then look at the student answers that follow.

Commentary on sample student answers

Read the comments (preceded by the icon **e**) showing how many marks each answer would be awarded in the exam and exactly where marks are gained or lost.

■About this book

This student guide on US/comparative politics will help you to improve your knowledge, understanding and skill in relation to the Edexcel A-level Politics Paper 3. It covers an outline of all the key topic material, an explanation of the key assessment requirements of Paper 3, as well as student answers to exam-style questions together with examiner comments.

The **Content Guidance** section deals with all the topics and all the main areas you need to understand, as outlined in the Edexcel A-level specification. The main topics are:

■ US Constitution and federalism
■ US Congress
■ US presidency
■ US Supreme Court and civil rights
■ US democracy and participation

You can use this section to familiarise yourself with all the key ideas, arguments and concepts. It also provides you with a range of relevant evidence which you can use. As well as knowing all the key facts, you will also need to be able to both analyse and evaluate key information. This is covered in the Content Guidance, but the Questions & Answers section will give you a more detailed awareness of what is required.

The A-level examination requires you to be able to compare the US and UK systems in specific areas of each topic. This includes key similarities as well as differences between the politics of the two countries. The requirement does not cover all parts of each topic, only those which are specified by the Edexcel examination board. Each topic chapter in this guide has a comparative section, which makes clear what you need to know. Before tackling the comparative sections it is important that you have studied the relevant UK topic beforehand (these are assessed in Papers 1 and 2).

The **Questions & Answers** section outlines how the examination board will assess your answers. It also provides you with a range of answers of different standards, with examiner-style comments. This will help you to understand what a successful answer requires.

This guide is just that — a concise outline of what you need to know. For more detailed information you can use other A-level politics textbooks such as those by Anthony Bennett or Andrew Colclough. You also need to be aware of the ever-changing nature of the US and UK political systems and maintain an awareness of contemporary developments. You can do this online via media outlets such as the *Washington Post*, *New York Times* or *Politico*. In addition, there are some excellent online politics resources aimed at updating A-level politics students. Articles from *Politics Review* or the latest posts from the LGS politics blog — https://lgspolitics.wordpress.com/ — can help with both the theory and the latest evidence.

We hope you enjoy US/comparative politics as much as we do and hope that this book adds to both your appreciation and success.

Content Guidance

■ US Constitution and federalism

The nature of the US Constitution

The creation of the US Constitution at the Philadelphia Convention, and its ratification in 1789, forged the 13 formerly British colonies into the new, sovereign country of the United States of America.

Vagueness, codification and entrenchment

At 7,000 words, the US Constitution is a short document, considering it outlined the new political system which would govern the USA. It is, therefore, vague in places while being specific in others. The codified document is divided into seven articles, with the subsequent addition of 27 amendments, and outlines the powers of each branch of government and how the new country would operate as a democracy.

Some of the powers given to federal government are explicit within the Constitution, while some powers exercised by government today are as a result of the vague nature of the Constitution.

- Enumerated powers are those which are explicitly laid out in the Constitution and given to a branch of government: for example, Congress is given the power to ratify treaties and the president is given the right to veto bills from Congress.
- Implied powers are those which are taken and exercised by a branch of government without it having been given this power explicitly: for example, the 'necessary and proper clause', which allows Congress far greater scope over what laws it may pass.

The US Constitution is entrenched, ensuring that it cannot be easily changed. Importantly, the Constitution requires a clear majority, a 'supermajority', in order for any amendment to be added to it. This makes the process more challenging and is one of the reasons so few amendments have been added in over 200 years.

The (powers) of the US branches of government

The first three articles of the Constitution outline the enumerated powers of the three branches that make up the federal government of the USA. The main powers of each branch are:

- Congress (Article I): all legislative power; power to lay and collect taxes; regulate commerce; coin money; declare war; veto override; impeachment; investigation; ratifying treaties and appointments (actually in Article II)

Constitution A set of principles and practices which outlines how a political system runs, the location of power and the relationship between the government and the governed.

Codification A constitution which is written into one document.

Knowledge check 1

Why is the 'necessary and proper clause' nicknamed the 'elastic clause'?

Entrenchment The system for amending the Constitution being protected by law; in the case of the US Constitution, amendment requires a two-thirds majority in Congress and support from three-quarters of the states.

Enumerated powers Powers which are explicitly listed and given to a branch of government in the Constitution.

- President (Article II): recommend legislation; sign or veto legislation; commander-in-chief; nomination of judges; power of pardon
- Supreme Court (Article III): judicial power

In separating the powers out in this way, and allowing each branch the power to check the actions of the others, the US Constitution should ensure that no one branch of government becomes too powerful.

The other articles deal with the role of the states (Article IV), the amendment process (Article V), the supremacy of the US Constitution to all other law (Article VI) and the ratification of the Constitution (Article VII).

The amendment process

Article V explains how amendments to the US Constitution can be made. The formal process is shown in Table 1.

The ability to amend the Constitution was crucial in getting the document ratified — a number of states refused to agree to this new constitution without certain changes being added. Although the Constitution was ratified in 1788, these changes were made in the Bill of Rights, which was added in 1791 and consisted of ten amendments which protected citizens' and states' rights more explicitly.

Table 1 The amendment process

Federal level — proposal stage	States level — ratification stage
Two-thirds of both Houses of Congress agree to propose an amendment	Three-quarters of state legislatures ratify the amendment
Two-thirds of states call a national constitutional convention, which proposes an amendment	Three-quarters of states hold state constitutional conventions and vote to ratify the amendment

There have been 27 amendments to the US Constitution:
- The Bill of Rights (1st–10th), which protects freedoms such as speech, religion and assembly, freedom from cruel and unusual punishment, and reserving all other powers not mentioned in the Constitution to the states
- The 12th, 20th, 22nd and 25th, which all clarify the presidential election and succession procedures
- The Civil War amendments (13th–15th), which ensure that recently freed slaves will be treated equally under the Constitution
- The 16th, which allows Congress to raise income tax and is the only amendment which overturned a Supreme Court ruling
- The 17th, which makes the role of senator elected rather than appointed
- The 18th and 21st, which respectively ban and then allow the production and sale of alcohol
- The 19th and 26th, which change voting eligibility, removing gender requirements and lowering the voting age to 18

Knowledge check 2

Where does the Supreme Court formally get the power of judicial review from?

Exam tip

Make sure that you are aware of the difference between 'separation of powers' and 'checks and balances', and how they relate to each other.

Advantages of the process

- The requirement for **supermajorities** ensures the broad support of the US population for any amendment.
- It protects the Constitution from being changed by a short-lived popular opinion.
- It prevents tyranny — of the larger states over the small by valuing each state equally in the process, and of the federal government by requiring state approval.
- It works — there have been amendments to the Constitution.

Disadvantages of the process

- The requirement for a supermajority makes it very difficult to pass any amendments, meaning the Constitution may become outdated.
- The requirement for supermajorities makes it possible to ignore minority interests.
- Mistakes have been made — the 18th Amendment, later repealed by the 21st Amendment, shows the process is not rigorous enough.
- It is possible for a small number of states to prevent an amendment passing, even if it is supported by a majority of the US population.

The principles of the US Constitution

The Founding Fathers wrote the US Constitution using a number of key **principles** that are evident in the text of the document (even if the word itself does not appear). These 'principles' were essentially the beliefs the Founding Fathers were trying to protect in their newly independent country.

Federalism

A **federal** government is one in which two levels of government exist, with both having their own powers. In the US Constitution, these two levels are 'federal' (or national) government and the state governments.

The word 'federal' or '**federalism**' does not actually appear in the US Constitution but the principle is embedded throughout the document in the way that power is divided. The Constitution tries to protect the powers of each level of government in a number of ways. These are shown in Table 2.

Table 2 How the Constitution protects the power of the states and federal government

Protecting the power of states	Protecting the power of federal government
■ 10th Amendment ■ The states control the running of elections ■ Frequent, staggered election cycle ■ States appoint their senators	■ Enumerated powers in Articles I, II and III ■ Implied powers such as the 'elastic clause' ■ The power to raise tax so federal government would be funded

Supermajority The requirement to gain a required level of support which exceeds a standard majority of 50% + 1.

Exam tip

To achieve AO2 analysis, you must explain *why* these points could be considered an advantage or a disadvantage. Do not just describe them.

Principle A basic idea which provides the framework for US democracy and is embedded within the US Constitution.

Knowledge check 3

Who were the Founding Fathers?

Federalism The sharing of sovereignty between the federal (or national) government and the states, where each one has its own areas of power and responsibility.

The powers of federal government are enumerated in the Constitution; any powers that are not listed here were expected to be carried out by the state governments. The addition of the 10th Amendment in 1791 made this expectation clear:

> **The powers not delegated to the United States by the Constitution, nor prohibited by it to the States, are reserved to the States respectively, or to the people.**

In the event of disagreement between the federal and state governments over the exercise of these powers, the Supreme Court would be the body that decided on the outcome.

Federalism can also be seen in the requirement for both national and state level approval for amendments to the Constitution (see Table 1), and in giving the states the power to choose their own two senators to send to national government.

Separation of powers and checks and balances

In order to ensure that the newly independent country would remain free from the tyranny they had seen under the British, the Founding Fathers applied the principle of 'separation of powers' within the Constitution (see Table 3). This means that each of the three branches of government must remain completely independent of the others, be selected by different processes and no one is allowed to be a member of more than one branch. This would prevent any one branch holding too much power and would require cooperation between the branches for government to work. President Obama, along with Vice President Biden and three other senators, all had to resign their seats in the Senate in order to take up posts in the executive branch in 2009.

Table 3 Separation of powers

Theoretical name	Legislature	Executive	Judiciary
Theoretical role	Create law	Execute law	Interpret law
US name	Congress	President	Supreme Court

In addition to simply dividing up the powers of government between these three branches, the Founding Fathers also gave each branch the ability to limit the actions of another branch. This would ensure no one branch became dominant over the others. This is known as checks and balances, of which the key examples are as follows.

Checks by Congress

- Override the presidential veto by a two-thirds vote in *both* Houses of Congress
- 'Power of the purse' — Congress, as the representatives of the taxpayers, controls the budget and therefore any money that the president is allocated
- The Senate can ratify or reject treaties and appointments (to federal offices or courts) put to them by the president
- Congress can impeach the president for 'treason, bribery, or other high crimes and misdemeanors'

Separation of powers
The division of government into the separate bodies — legislature (Congress), executive (president) and judiciary (Supreme Court) — each with its own powers, personnel and buildings.

Knowledge check 4

The principle of 'separation of powers' comes from which political philosopher?

Checks and balances
The division of powers to each branch of government, allowing branches to prevent another branch from acting.

Checks by the president

- Veto any legislation from Congress
- Recommend legislation to Congress at the State of the Union address
- Power of the pardon
- Nomination of federal officers and justices

Checks by the Supreme Court

- Judicial review

Bipartisanship

The Founding Fathers were not in favour of political parties, but some of them seemed to believe that the formation of parties was inevitable. The Constitution was not written with parties in mind, but it does have some safeguards which prevent them being too powerful. It allows for different groups to control different branches, but forces them to work together. While the word 'bipartisanship' does not appear in the Constitution, the concept is evident in a number of ways:

- The staggered election cycle, with the House of Representatives elected every 2 years, the president every 4 years and the Senate every 6 years (although one-third of senators are re-elected every 2 years), means a different party could control each branch of government and forces representatives to be frequently accountable to their constituents.
- Supermajorities are required in some circumstances, such as for constitutional amendments and to override the presidential veto; this requires party cooperation.
- The checks and balances written in the Constitution mean that in order to achieve anything, the different branches of government must work together.

Limited government

The Founding Fathers wanted to create a government that could not limit the freedoms of its citizens and would not become too large or overbearing. Like 'federalism', the phrase 'limited government' does not appear in the Constitution. Throughout the Constitution, however, there are requirements which stop the government from acting how it wishes — they *limit* what the government can do.

The most obvious limits on the federal government are the systems of separation of powers and checks and balances, which limit the actions that each branch can take. In addition, the Bill of Rights (1st–10th Amendments) was ratified in 1791 to protect the basic freedoms of citizens, including other freedoms that might not be explicitly laid out in the Constitution (in the 9th Amendment).

The main characteristics of US federalism

The USA is a large and diverse nation; many of the states have their own culture, heritage and distinct identity. This was true at the time the Constitution was written, and the Founding Fathers had to strike a balance between a national government that could defend the country and allowing each state to have its own power. Federalism tried to allow for this compromise, as outlined above.

Exam tip

The effectiveness of checks and balances changes over time depending on a range of factors, such as divided government or approval ratings. Avoid simply stating that the system 'works' or 'does not work'.

Bipartisanship When two opposing parties work together to achieve one policy or initiative.

Limited government A government which is subject to limitations on its actions and powers over its citizens.

Knowledge check 5

How does the Constitution protect government from popular consent?

Knowledge check 6

Where in the Constitution are the rights of states protected?

Exam tip

In demonstrating that the USA *is* federal today, you will need examples — such as North Carolina's transgender bathroom law, Texas HB2 on abortion or various states' marijuana legalisation.

The nature of the federal system of government and its relationship with the states

There is no absolute division between state and federal government in the Constitution; while each is given some powers, the vagueness of the document allows for a degree of uncertainty. The Constitution tried to ensure the delicate balance of federalism would be protected. However, the interpretation of the Constitution in the years following its ratification established that the federal government was, in effect, supreme over the states:

- *Fletcher* v *Peck* (1810) established precedent allowing the Supreme Court (federal government) to strike down state laws.
- *McCulloch* v *Maryland* (1819) established precedent that states could not prevent federal government from using its constitutional powers.
- *Gibbons* v *Ogden* (1824) established that Congress could control trade between the states, using the 'commerce clause' within the Constitution.

In each of these landmark cases, the Supreme Court ruled in favour of the federal government over the states, a trend which some may argue has continued into the twenty-first century. However, the relationship between federal government and state governments has changed over time:

- Dual federalism (1787–1930s) — state and federal governments exercised a roughly equal amount of power but in completely separate areas. While the federal government did challenge states at times (see above) the emphasis during this period was on states running their own domestic affairs.
- Cooperative federalism (1930s–1960s) — the division between state and federal responsibility became blurred. Federal government grew larger in response to events such as the Great Depression and the Second World War, taking on some policy areas previously controlled by states.
- New federalism (1960s onwards) — attempts to try and return some of the powers taken by federal government to the states.

The relationship between the states and federal government today is complex and not easily characterised by one theory.

Knowledge check 7

What does the power of judicial review allow the US Supreme Court to do?

Exam tip

Having a basic knowledge of the different types of federalism will allow you to compare the extent of federalism in the USA today. Comparing change over time is a key analytical (AO2) skill.

Case study

The complex federal–state relationship with marijuana

In 1970, a congressional law, the Controlled Substances Act, made marijuana a federally illegal Class I drug in the USA. The 'supremacy clause' of the Constitution makes it clear that federal law trumps state law, therefore marijuana is still illegal today in the whole of the USA. This can be enforced by federal agencies such as the Drug Enforcement Agency (DEA).

From 1973, however, there has been a growing acceptance of marijuana use within some states — this began by decriminalising it (Oregon, 1973), then allowing its use for medicinal purposes (California, 1996) before finally allowing it for recreational purposes (Colorado, 2012). In these circumstances, the state law and federal law is in direct conflict,

→

with marijuana still being illegal at a federal level but legal at state level.

Where a state has legalised marijuana use for any reason, the people of that state using it are at risk of being raided by a federal law enforcement agency for breaking federal law. However, local law enforcement, which is run by the state, enforces the law of the individual state and therefore will not prosecute these people for marijuana use.

The growing number of states legalising marijuana use puts pressure on the federal government to change its law too. In August 2013, the US Justice Department issued guidelines showing it would focus on prosecuting marijuana use in limited circumstances, such as when firearms were involved. Other than this, in states where marijuana was legal, federal agencies would have little involvement.

In 2016 a record nine states had marijuana laws on the ballot, including five states which asked whether recreational marijuana should be legalised in their state — California, Massachusetts, Nevada and Maine voters cast their ballot in favour of marijuana. Today, eight states have legalised recreational use, and twenty-eight have legalised medicinal use; federally, however, marijuana remains an illegal Class I drug.

Examples such as the legal status of marijuana demonstrate the blurred lines between state and federal power today; both retain some power but both equally have influence (if not actual power) over the other.

Under Obama

Obama's focus on domestic policy, such as the Patient Protection and Affordable Care Act (Obamacare) and gun control, considerably changed the nature of the federal–state relationship. Much like cooperative federalism, the Obama administration blurred the lines between the responsibilities of states and federal government. However, like new federalism, there were areas where the administration built within this a protection for individual states' rights. These examples show both federal and state power:

- Obamacare made it mandatory for states to provide 'healthcare exchanges', from which citizens could purchase healthcare insurance. However, the details on how these exchanges were to be set up and run were largely left for each state to determine. Additionally, the federal government would cover most of the additional cost of this expansion (covering 100% until 2020, and 90% thereafter), therefore not burdening the states with this cost.
- The Recovery Act was a $787 billion stimulus package following the 2008 recession. One-third of this was given to state governments, more than any previous such bill. The Race to the Top initiative was funded by this Act and aimed to improve the quality of education. As well as allowing states to exercise this power, it also allowed local school districts, such as Houston, to bid for money, even if their state did not.
- In 2009, Obama issued a memorandum undoing the Bush-era policy of pre-emption. This policy used federal regulations to override states, whereas Obama directed his federal agencies to override states 'only with full consideration of the legitimate prerogatives of the states and with a sufficient legal basis for pre-emption'.
- The Supreme Court protected states' power in some areas (gun control) and federal government power in others (Obamacare, gay marriage).

Federalism today

While the federal–state relationship is constantly changing, depending on national circumstances and the administration, some things do remain clear today:

Exam tip

Knowing a few examples well, like this case study, is more important than knowing the name of lots of examples. To gain analytical (AO2) marks, you need to show the relationship of an example to your theory; you cannot do this by just name-dropping examples.

Exam tip

Almost every action by any branch of federal government has an impact on states. Pick key *recent* policies from Bush, Obama and Trump and show how they both took away and protected states' rights — such policies rarely only do one of these!

- Federal government controls foreign policy, including war and treaties.
- The use of the 'commerce clause' in the Constitution has allowed federal government greater control over the states in domestic policy.
- The enforcement of federal law largely relies on state law enforcement and courts.
- The Supreme Court has the power to change or uphold legislation at state level.
- The nature of US federalism has led to an incredibly complex legal system, economic system and court system, with punishments, taxes and public policy varying considerably between states.
- The size of the USA, geographically and in terms of population, means that states and local governments retain considerable control over the daily lives of citizens.
- The diversity of the USA continues to develop — it is projected that by 2060, Hispanic-Americans will make up 28.6% of the US population.

Knowledge check 8

What is the 'commerce clause'?

Interpretations and debates around the US Constitution and federalism

The extent of democracy within the US Constitution

Before judging the extent of democracy within the Constitution, it is important to understand different types of democracy. The two key types to review are liberal democracy and representative democracy.

- Liberal democracy — in which equality of rights, protection of rights, and free and fair elections are of paramount importance
- Representative democracy — in which people elect officials to represent them in institutions of government. The Burkean model of representative democracy also suggests that these representatives should act as trustees not delegates.

In these terms, the US Constitution does largely advance both a liberal and a representative democracy, while aspects of the Constitution seem opposed to these ideals. This is set out in Tables 4 and 5.

Knowledge check 9

What is the difference between a trustee and a delegate?

Table 4 The US Constitution and representative democracy

How the US Constitution upholds representative democracy	How the US Constitution opposes representative democracy
<ul><li>The House of Representatives is elected directly by citizens of each state</li><li>The House of Representatives is elected roughly in proportion, equalising representation — every 10 years a census reapportions seats in the House based on the movement of population. In 2010, Texas gained four seats, while New York lost two</li><li>The frequent election cycle means that congressmen have to pay close attention to their voters. The House of Representatives is wholly re-elected every 2 years, and senators serve 6 years with one-third of the Senate re-elected every 2 years</li><li>Amendments have upheld representative democracy; senators are now elected, while women and those aged 18 or over can vote</li></ul>	<ul><li>Senators were unelected until 1913</li><li>Having two senators per state means representation varies by state population — Wyoming has two senators for approximately half a million people; California has two senators for approximately 40 million people</li><li>Having at least one House of Representatives member per state means the level of representation also varies — in the 2010 census, the average Montana district had approximately 1 million people in it; the average Rhode Island district had approximately half a million</li><li>The Electoral College limits the impact of the public vote on the outcome — the election winners in 2000 and 2016 did not reflect the popular vote</li></ul>

Table 5 The US Constitution and liberal democracy

How the US Constitution upholds liberal democracy	How the US Constitution opposes liberal democracy
■ Key rights are protected by the Constitution for *all* citizens — the 1st Amendment alone protects free speech, press, assembly and religion ■ The Constitution sets out the rules for elections, including terms, electors and control over elections — the frequent election cycle of every 2 years allows for a high level of accountability ■ The separation of powers should protect rights and prevent tyranny of the government — the Supreme Court has struck down state and federal law to protect gay rights	■ The requirement for supermajorities can lead to tyranny of the majority — women and minority groups have all had rights restricted ■ The protection of rights for minorities has largely been left to the Supreme Court but it has no power of enforcement. The Court ruled against segregation in schools in 1954, yet Mississippi was still receiving similar rulings in 2016 ■ Leaving election practices in the hands of states has led to wide variation. While nearly half of Americans live in districts using paper ballots, one-quarter use electronic voting, which has led to claims of election fraud

Exam tip

'Democracy' is a term that needs consideration. In an exam, you should not use it in a superficial way, but instead try to reference which type of democracy you are discussing. The two most commonly discussed are representative and liberal, so know these well.

Judiciable The ability of the Supreme Court to judge the actions of the government (federal and state), using the Constitution as the basis for this judgement.

Strengths and weaknesses of the US Constitution

The strengths and weaknesses of the Constitution are rarely clear cut — instead it is a matter of how the nature of the Constitution can be interpreted, as shown in Table 6.

Table 6 Strengths and weaknesses of the US Constitution

Nature	Strength	Weakness
Codified	The principles of government are clearly set out and the document is judiciable (AO1), making it difficult for any branch to become tyrannical (AO2) Example: Executive orders	The Constitution is more rigid and therefore can become outdated (AO1), which can make aspects of the document irrelevant to modern life (AO2) Example: 2nd Amendment
Vagueness	The vague nature of the Constitution ensures that its meaning can be reinterpreted over time (AO1). This has overcome the need for formal amendments (AO2) Example: Abortion	Branches of government can take advantage of the vagueness, which could allow them to expand their power (AO1), thereby diminishing the power given to other branches in the Constitution (AO2) Example: Power to declare war
Amendment process	Article V allows for amendments and clearly works, given that there have been 27 amendments (AO1). This means the Constitution can be updated to respond to the wishes of the population in a representative democracy (AO2) Example: 26th Amendment	The amendment process is not only incredibly slow, but also allows for minority rights and values to be ignored (AO1). This means that the Constitution may be considered outdated and therefore less relevant today (AO2) Example: 27th Amendment took 202 years to pass

→

Nature	Strength	Weakness
Separation of powers	In clearly giving each branch of government enumerated powers, the Constitution provides each branch with guaranteed powers as well as checks on other branches (AO1). This ensures that government remains limited, well scrutinised and responsive to the wishes of the governed (AO2) Example: Obama and Obamacare	The division of powers in this way often leads to gridlock (AO1). This means that government is fundamentally not fulfilling its function of governing, which undermines its power (AO2) Example: 2013 shutdown
Federalism	In guaranteeing certain powers to states through the 10th Amendment, the Constitution upholds the principle of federalism (AO1). This protects the rights and diversity of the states in an increasingly globalised world where federal government has grown considerably (AO2) Example: Obama and immigration	Despite protections in the Constitution, the rights of states have been eroded by federal policy and the power of the Supreme Court (AO1). As the USA has grown to over 300 million people, protecting individual rights has often come at the cost of the identity of individual states Example: Gay rights

When evaluating strengths and weaknesses, it is often useful to consider what the Constitution was meant to do. From this, it is possible to debate the ways in which it is effective at achieving this or not.

Impact on the US government today

The US Constitution not only outlines how government should work, but places considerable constraints on it too. It is important to recognise that this is not about strengths and weaknesses, but about *government*. Crucially, this is not a historical assessment — the impact must be measured 'today'. Therefore, there must be evidence from recent years that supports each impact. Most 'impacts' will be assessed as positive impacts or negative impacts.

Positive impacts

- Each branch of government is given explicit powers which cannot be removed, ensuring each branch remains relevant, even in times of **divided government**.
- Frequent elections forces representatives to listen to their constituents, ensuring legitimacy of government.
- The acceptance of judicial review means that disagreements can be settled in the Supreme Court.
- The necessity for branches to work together through checks and balances means that majority interests are usually upheld, which should increase support for government.

Negative impacts

- Separation of powers and checks and balances can lead to gridlock, meaning government is not governing.
- Federalism means that sovereignty is shared and not only reduces the power given to federal government but also allows states to sue the federal government.

Exam tip

It is crucial to be able to explain *why* each of these points is a strength or weakness — this is AO2. Make sure you can explain what actually happened in each example, and *why* it is relevant to the point. What does it demonstrate?

Divided government
A situation where one of either the president, the House of Representatives or the Senate is controlled by a different party to the others.

- The role of judicial review means minorities or minority views have been able to stall the functions of government.
- The vagueness of the Constitution has meant 'loopholes' have been exploited, such as executive orders, allowing for the dominance of one branch over another.

In assessing the impact 'today', the circumstances of government are key. If federal government is controlled by one party, if there has been a national disaster, or if a president has just been elected, often federal government is more effective. In times of divided government, in times of low approval ratings, or in the later years of a presidency, the impact of the Constitution is often more negative.

The debates around the extent to which the USA remains federal today

While the focus of international news is often the institutions of federal government in the USA, the role of state governments in everyday life is crucial. In 2012, while there was one federal government and 50 state governments, there were 90,056 local governments — this highlights the extent of federalism within the USA. This has a variety of consequences:

- The rights of citizens vary between states — for example, the driving age, the age of consent or the right to use marijuana.
- Criminal punishments differ between states — 32 states have the death penalty as a legal form of punishment, with five different methods of execution (lethal injection, electric chair, hanging, firing squad and gas chamber).
- Politically, elections in each state are run according to state rules. This means some states, although not many, still use punch cards, while others use electronic voting or paper ballots.
- Taxes vary massively across each state — sales tax, income tax and property tax not only vary in the amount claimed by each state, but also in whether they are collected by the state itself or by a local government.
- In a judicial sense, not only is the court system different across each state, the states have used the federal court system to effectively challenge for their own rights. Obamacare, abortion and immigration were all challenged by states in the Supreme Court.

It is important to recognise the reliance that federal government has on state governments. Even in policies such as Obamacare, there are sections which rely on states and allow for each state to interpret and apply law as it sees fit. Understanding some key examples of congressional law and how they have either been accepted or rejected by states is crucial.

Comparisons with the UK

The nature (codified/uncodified) of the constitutions and their sources, provisions and principles

The main differences between the constitutions of the USA and the UK are shown in Table 7.

Exam tip

Beware not to ignore words such as 'today' or 'now' in exam questions. They are asking you to review a topic with specific focus on recent years, not a description of history. To reach the top levels, a student must use modern examples and compare these to the expected roles and powers laid out in the Constitution.

Exam tip

When comparing the US and UK Constitutions, it is important not only to identify what the differences are, but also why these differences exist or what the impact of these differences are. This will help you gain AO2 marks in 12-mark questions.

Table 7 Key differences between the US and UK constitutions

UK Constitution	US Constitution
Uncodified — therefore flexible and easily changed	Codified — therefore protected by law and safe from manipulation by government
Sources — as it is uncodified, the UK Constitution is found across a range of sources, including statute law, common law and works of authority	Sources — the main source of the Constitution is the document itself, consisting of 7,000 words. The 27 amendments and subsequent Supreme Court interpretive amendments also form part of the Constitution
Fused powers — this allows for the dominance of government over Parliament, what Hailsham referred to as an 'elective dictatorship'	Separation of powers — which prevents one branch from becoming dominant by dividing powers between them, but which can result in gridlock
Limited checks and balances — the new UK Supreme Court has been more willing to challenge government, as has the reformed House of Lords, but ultimately the balance of power resides with government	Clear checks and balances — the power of each branch to prevent the work of another largely encourages a collegiate effort to govern. However, this can result in gridlock or, worse, a circumvention of these checks
Devolution — see text below	Federalism — see text below
Sovereignty — resides in Parliament, at least in theory, not in the Constitution. This allows Parliament, and therefore effectively the government, considerable power	Sovereignty — resides in the document which delegates powers to federal and state governments. The Supreme Court also has quasi-sovereignty as the only body which can interpret the sovereign Constitution

The US federal system and the UK system of devolution

The key difference between federalism and devolution is the direction in which power flows. In federalism, power flows up from the states to federal government to allow this body power, whereas, in devolution, power flows down from the central government to create devolved bodies which exist only by the allowance of this government.

Similarities

- In both countries, regional differences occur in policy areas. In the UK, tuition fees vary by country and in the USA marijuana laws vary by state.
- In both countries, the central government retains control over policy areas of national interest. The power to declare war resides in the national government of both the UK and the USA.
- In both countries, the central government and regional governments have experienced disagreements. Scotland has considerable disagreement with the UK policy of Brexit, while Texas objected to, and won against, federal government immigration policy.
- In both countries, the law from central government is superior to regional laws, particularly if the two come into conflict.

Differences

- In the USA, the states have sovereignty given by the Constitution, guaranteeing their power. In the UK, the devolved assemblies exist only due to parliamentary statute, which could be revoked by a future Parliament.

- The judiciable nature of the US Constitution means states can directly challenge federal government. In the UK, while this is possible, the lack of sovereignty of Supreme Court decisions makes this dependent on Parliament following any ruling.
- Sovereignty in the devolved bodies of the UK has not been equally shared, with each body being given different rights and responsibilities, while all states in the USA are equally sovereign.

Rational, cultural and structural approaches

Rational, cultural and structural approaches are lenses through which the similarities and differences between the US and UK constitutions can be understood. Each theory can be used to try and explain the same point.

- **Rational theory** suggests that outcomes can be explained by individuals acting selfishly.
- **Cultural theory** suggests that outcomes can be explained by people acting on a shared belief or ideology.
- **Structural theory** suggests that outcomes can be explained by the institutions and systems of government.

Most of the differences and similarities between the UK and US Constitutions are best understood structurally. Most differences that exist do so because of the systems and processes laid out in each constitution — the amendment process, the allocation of power, devolution and federalism, and so on. These processes outline exactly how power is to be distributed and used, which is the root of many of the similarities and differences between each country — for example, the extent of checks and balances differs due to the nature of each constitution (codified and uncodified) and the location of sovereignty.

There is also a clear cultural aspect to the differences and similarities, however. The UK Constitution has a long and evolutionary history, whereas the US Constitution was created more quickly as a response to a situation. The result has been that the 'shared beliefs' of each nation vary due to their experience. For example, the shared belief in Scottish nationalism and the SNP resulted in the independence referendum in 2014; US states may have a similar level of shared beliefs depending on their region. However, a shared belief in limited government and fear of tyranny in the USA underpin the clear separation of powers, whereas the UK's fused powers are accepted by the population with little public pressure for change.

The rational aspect has limited relevance to this topic, as there are few individuals to act selfishly. However, it could be applied when explaining the difference in federalism or separation of powers as a frequent election cycle means congressmen are often more responsive to their constituents than to their parties, underpinning state power. Comparatively, UK MPs perhaps owe more to their party rather than their constituency and therefore are more likely to support their party in Parliament, underpinning the unitary system in the UK.

Exam tip

These three theories only appear in question 2. You must be able to explain your answer by using at least one of them — be aware that not every theory fits every difference or similarity. Know the definitions well.

Summary

- The US Constitution is the source of all power and the location of ultimate sovereignty in the USA. Despite its age and the disagreements and problems it has created, it remains central to every aspect of government in the USA.
- The key principles may not be explicitly named within the document but are clearly woven throughout the articles and amendments. The values of federalism and limited government often form the core of Supreme Court cases brought by states against the government. Bipartisanship, checks and balances and separation of powers should ensure that government works together in the interest of the people but can equally achieve the exact opposite, and at the extremes create gridlock and a complete lack of governance.
- The difficulty in the amendment process should not be confused with a lack of amendments — the interpretative amendments of the Supreme Court, coupled with the vagueness of the document, have allowed for considerable development over time within the Constitution.
- The states remain a crucial vehicle for carrying out federal government policy and have a vast impact on the daily life of citizens despite the erosion of state power and growth of federal government.
- The Constitution as written by the Founding Fathers produced a 'republic' rather than a 'democracy'. It is important to recognise that there are aspects of this document that therefore seemingly work against principles of liberal or representative democracy.

■ US Congress

The structure of Congress

Bicameral nature

The Founding Fathers ensured that Congress had two chambers, the House of Representatives and the Senate. Congress was thereby able to apply a number of key principles required by the framers:

- Checks and balances, in which checks took place *within* the legislative branch as well as *between* the executive, legislature and judiciary
- The creation of different term lengths, providing different types of representation within Congress, with senators (6-year term) being far less sensitive to public opinion than members of the House of Representatives (2-year term)
- Protection of state interests — the driving force behind the creation of a Senate in which all states were given an equal number of politicians, regardless of population

The membership of Congress

There are minor differences in the constitutional requirements for membership of each of the two chambers of Congress. While senators are required to be at least 30 years of age and to have been a citizen for 9 years, members of the House need only be 25 and to have been a citizen for 7 years. Other differences between the two are listed in Table 8.

Table 8 Main differences between the House and Senate

The House of Representatives		The Senate
435	**Total membership**	100
Representative (the term 'congressman' or 'congresswoman' usually refers to a member of the House only)	**Title of member**	Senator
2 years	**Term length**	6 years
District	**Constituency**	State
Roughly proportional to population (with Wyoming having one and California having 53)	**Number per state**	Two (each senator represents the whole state)

The most powerful person in the House is the speaker. This is a political position, with the House majority party choosing the speaker to act as its leader. The speaker attempts to unify the party and provide policy leadership, often determining the agenda of the majority party and therefore the House in general.

The House majority leader is best viewed as the speaker's deputy. The minority leader in each chamber heads the minority party (Democrats in each chamber in the 115th Congress). These minority leaders will aim to become speaker (House) or majority leader (Senate) after future congressional elections.

Table 9 details the membership of Congress as of 2017.

Exam tip

Make sure you are familiar with several important politicians in Congress. By researching the figures in Table 9, you will gain greater depth of understanding and be more able to remember who they are.

Table 9 Composition of Congress 2017–18

The speaker of the House of Representatives — Paul Ryan The House majority leader — Kevin McCarthy House minority leader — Nancy Pelosi	**Key positions in the 115th Congress**	President of the Senate — Mike Pence Senate majority leader — Mitch McConnell Senate minority leader — Charles Schumer
Democrat 194 Republican 241	**Party control**	Democrat 46 Republican 52 Independent 2

The election cycle

House and Senate elections take place every 2 years, using first past the post (FPTP). All members of the House are elected every 2 years, and approximately a third of senators are elected every 2 years. While all senators are elected for a 6-year term, by staggering Senate elections the composition of the Senate (including the party majority) can be altered at frequent intervals.

Midterm elections take place every 4 years, and are often seen as a referendum on the first 2 years of a presidency. While the president is not on the ballot, many voters use these elections to provide a check on the president's agenda, with the president's party typically facing defeat, losing seats, if not always its overall majority. Only three US presidents (F. D. Roosevelt, W. Clinton and G. W. Bush) have been in office when their party increased its seats in at least one chamber. Midterm elections are highly significant because of the impact of their result:

Midterm election Any election, particularly for Congress, held in the middle of a president's term.

- The president can experience a major decline in power.
- Midterms can lead to a change in policy direction of the country.
- They can lead to legislative **gridlock** between president and Congress.

In the midterms of 2010 the Democrats lost control of the House, leaving Obama to face a hostile majority. As a result Obama found it much harder to achieve his legislative goals. In these elections, the GOP (Grand Old Party, the Republican Party) developed a national agenda, The Pledge to America, giving Speaker-elect John Boehner a mandate for change. This, alongside the loss of Democrat control of the Senate in the 2014 midterms, contributed to legislative gridlock, in which Congress repeatedly blocked Obama's agenda. The failure of the two sides to agree on budget issues led to the 16-day federal government shutdown in 2013.

The distribution of powers within Congress

Some congressional powers are awarded to one chamber only and are referred to as exclusive powers. Other powers are concurrent; they are held by the House and Senate.

The exclusive powers of each chamber — the House

- **To impeach.** This occurs when the House brings formal charges against any public official. The charges cannot be justified on political grounds but must relate to treason, bribery or a high crime or misdemeanour. Two presidents (Andrew Johnson in 1868 and Bill Clinton in 1998) have been impeached by the two-thirds vote required.
- **To elect the president if no candidate receives over 50% of the Electoral College.** In this scenario each state is given one vote in the House of Representatives to determine who the president will be. The power can be considered insignificant in the sense that it is unlikely to be used. It has only been used twice, in 1800 and 1824.
- **To begin consideration of money bills.** All revenue-raising bills, those which impose taxes, have to pass through the House first. This is in contrast to other bills, which can pass through either chamber first and are often dealt with concurrently. This is a limited power with all House decisions being submitted to the Senate, which can amend or reject.

The exclusive powers of each chamber — the Senate

- **To try an impeached official.** If the House impeaches a public official then it is the role of the Senate to hold a trial. A two-thirds Senate vote will subsequently remove the official from office. While Clinton was impeached, he was not removed from office, mainly because of the result of the midterm elections in 1998. Samuel Chase is the only Supreme Court justice to be impeached *and* removed from office (1804).
- **To ratify treaties**. The Senate has the power to accept or reject treaties negotiated by the president. Obama successfully achieved the two-thirds vote required for ratification when he secured a nuclear limitation deal with Russia (START Treaty) in 2010 but failed to convince a Republican-led Senate to back his treaty on disabled rights (2012). The use of executive agreements by the president, in which the president makes an agreement between himself and another country, could be used to bypass the need for Senate ratification.

Gridlock A situation in which decisions cannot be made because Congress and the president cannot come to an agreement. This often means that new laws cannot be passed.

Knowledge check 10

What is the difference between midterm elections and congressional elections?

- **To confirm presidential appointments.** With over 1,200 positions being scrutinised and voted on by the Senate, this exclusive power marks a major limitation on the power of the president. After investigations and committee hearings, the Senate can confirm a presidential nomination with a 50%+ vote. Some senior members of EXOP (the Executive Office of the President) and all federal judges and cabinet members have to be ratified. Having a Republican Senate majority made it easier (than would have been the case if the Democrats had gained control of the Senate in 2016) for President Trump to successfully achieve several controversial nominations such as Jeff Sessions (Attorney General) and Betsy DeVos (Education Secretary).

The exclusive powers of the Senate can be seen as far more significant than those of the House. This is mainly because they can be used on a more regular basis and can have a huge impact on both presidential power and US public policy.

The concurrent powers of Congress

Congress is given the following concurrent powers by the Constitution:

- **Legislation.** Article I gives all legislative power to Congress with both chambers' approval required for legislation to be enacted. Congress can amend legislation and has the ability to reject presidential proposals for legislation.

  For example, in 2017, the American Healthcare Act, an attempt to reform Obamacare, was eventually accepted by a House vote but continued to struggle to gain support in the Senate. Without support from both chambers it would be impossible to repeal Obamacare.

- **Amending the Constitution.** This power is shared with the states, with two-thirds of each chamber of Congress being required to change the US Constitution.

- **To declare war.** While there is a constitutional ambiguity here, given the president's position as commander-in-chief, the Founding Fathers gave Congress the power to begin military conflict.

The functions of Congress

There are three main functions of Congress:

- Representation
- Legislation
- Oversight

Representation

The significance of incumbency

A standard feature of Congress is high **incumbency** re-election rates. Those in office have an extremely high chance of retaining their position if they stand for re-election. In the 2016 elections, incumbency re-election rates were 97% for the House and 90% for the Senate. Why are they so high?

The electoral system

The use of a first-past-the-post, winner-takes-all system leads to the creation of safe seats. The person in office continues to get re-elected because they represent a party which has dominant support in that constituency. Representative John Conyers

> **Knowledge check 11**
> What is the difference between impeachment and removal from office?

> **Incumbency** The person currently in office. This can be used to distinguish between the politician who holds office, such as a current president or member of Congress, and challengers for a political position.

(Democrat, Michigan), re-elected in 2016, has served in the House since 1965. Serving a predominantly Democrat district, Conyers will know that he has won re-election before any votes are cast.

Incumbency advantage

Being in office gives incumbents a number of benefits which their political rivals do not enjoy. Current politicians often have name recognition, which they can use to run more effective election campaigns. In addition, they can also make use of pork-barrel legislation, in which they propose or amend legislation that brings benefits to their constituency. Politicians with shipbuilding facilities or defence contractors based in their constituencies have strongly supported many amendments to defence legislation, for example. In 2016 congressional incumbents raised a combined $627.3 million compared with just $135.3 million raised by their challengers.

Gerrymandering

High incumbency re-election rates are compounded by the gerrymandering of House districts. Boundaries are largely drawn up by the party in control of the state legislature (not by an independent body). The dominant party can therefore maximise its chances of winning as many House seats as possible. This can be seen in the contrast in Pennsylvania election results between the 2008 and 2012 elections. Having taken control of the state legislature after 2008, Republicans were able to redraw boundaries to increase their success in the House despite similar voting patterns. This helps to explain why incumbency re-election rates are higher in the House than the Senate.

High incumbency re-election rates have been criticised because they have major negative implications for representation with a lack of competitive electoral races. The incumbent faces little threat of removal and therefore is not necessarily sensitive to public opinion. High incumbency could be seen as positive, however, because it means that experienced politicians hold office, with a stronger understanding of both the workings of the political system and the issues facing US society.

Factors affecting voting behaviour within Congress

When voting within Congress (for example on legislative measures) a politician will be influenced by different things. As well as their own personal ideology, there are three key factors:

Parties and caucuses

Partly as a result of natural ideological agreement, members of Congress often vote along party lines. Such partisan voting can also occur because of pressure from party leaders or a desire to limit the political success of the opposing party/ president. There has been a rise in partisan voting in Congress in recent years. On the other hand, party unity is limited by a number of political and constitutional features of the US system. The separation of powers, in particular, leads to weak party leaders who may find it difficult to control those who do not follow the party line. The first vote in the House of Representatives in 2017 saw the vast majority of Republicans vote against the publicly stated wishes of Speaker Paul Ryan and other GOP leaders regarding the reduction of the power of the House Ethics Committee. **Congressional caucuses** can also have a major influence on voting.

Knowledge check 12

What is an incumbent?

Congressional caucus A formal group of politicians typically choosing a leader and holding regular meetings. These caucuses are based on shared interests or ideologies such as the congressional black caucus or the congressional steel caucus. They are often bipartisan and work to pursue legislative goals.

Given the common interest or ideology of caucus members, it is likely that they will vote in the same way.

Constituency

Sensitivity to public opinion is particularly strong, given the separation of powers, which helps to make members of Congress more accountable to constituents than party leaders. The individual voting record of a member of Congress is often highlighted at election time (by both the candidate and their opponents), sometimes leading a politician to oppose the party line. In 2017 many Republicans in the House and Senate voted against Republican Party plans to repeal Obamacare because it did not reflect the interests of their constituents. In addition, the prevalence of pork-barrel legislation can be seen as an indicator of the need to please constituency views.

Pressure groups and lobbyists

Pressure groups are influential over politicians, not only due to their powers of persuasion but because they can mobilise key voter groups to support or oppose a congressional candidate. In addition, such groups provide funding for candidates who will need to show continued support for a cause if they are to retain access to campaign contributions. In 2013 the Senate failed to pass gun control measures despite overwhelming public support. Many member of Congress may have made an electoral calculation which suggested that the strength of feeling of NRA (National Rifle Association) members would have a greater impact on their election chances than the majority view. Professional lobbyists could also be influential because of their connections with current politicians and the lure of a potentially lucrative post with a lobbying firm once they leave Congress.

Legislation

The legislative process

The legislative process in the USA is complex. Rather than learning and remembering all the details of all stages of the process it is useful to learn some of its main features.

Key characteristics of the legislative process of Congress

- Congress is proactive, not simply reactive. While it often responds to presidential proposals, it is active in initiating legislation for itself. This can be seen with the many budgets developed by Congress in recent years, such as those developed by Paul Ryan or his 2016 tax reform plan, A Better Way.
- Congress is active rather than passive. Unlike legislatures in parliamentary systems which are often dominated by the executive, Congress regularly amends or defeats presidential proposals, as we saw with the Affordable Care Act, gun control and immigration reform under President Obama.
- Legislation has to be agreed by both the House and the Senate, which have co-equal legislative power. A bill cannot become law unless both chambers agree.
- There are many legislative hurdles within Congress, which give rise to many amendments and many failed bills. As well as having to achieve the support of over 50% in each main chamber, proposals have a series of committees to negotiate.
- The lack of party unity can make it difficult to pass legislation.

Knowledge check 13

Does 'caucus' have more than one meaning?

- The president is highly influential in legislation, often setting the agenda and possessing the power to veto bills. A two-thirds vote of each chamber is required to overturn a presidential veto.

Knowledge check 14

What are the main obstacles which prevent a bill from becoming a law?

Strengths and weaknesses of the process

The legislative process has been criticised for a number of reasons:

- It is slow to pass legislation, with excessive compromise and amendments.
- The process may lead to poor quality policy. Legislative output is based on a compromise of pet projects and ideological interests, which means ineffective legislation.
- The tendency to pork barrel most legislation increases the national debt with projects which are unnecessary or poor value for money. This could be a criticism from a fiscal conservative position. It is also often used by liberals who regret the huge subsidies awarded to major corporations, viewing this as evidence of elitism in lawmaking.
- The weakness of the process has been exacerbated by a rise in partisanship. High party unity and unwillingness to compromise have increased the difficulty in passing legislation.

On the other hand, there are a number of strengths:

- The process reflects the desire of the Founding Fathers to prevent tyranny by ensuring a compromise of different interests. This encourages greater pluralism in decision making.
- Preventing legislation from passing could be seen as desirable, promoting the conservative values of limited government.
- Such a deliberative process should lead to higher quality policy by preventing rushed decisions.
- The legislative process does much to respect the important traditions of individual and state rights.

Legislative differences between the chambers

Each chamber has the ability to create its own procedures (within the Constitution), which has led to differences (see Table 10). In general, the House is more ordered and more subject to leadership influence than the Senate. This tends to mean that it is more difficult to pass legislation in the Senate compared to the House.

Table 10 Legislative differences between the House and the Senate

House	Senate
Amendments to legislation have to be *germane* to the bill under discussion. This means that amendments must be relevant to the proposed Act	While the germaneness rule applies to some bills in the Senate (such as appropriations), amendments can be added to most bills on unrelated matters. In 2016 the bill to address the Zika crisis was partly rejected by Democrats because of several amendments added by GOP senators to limit abortion
The legislative process is largely controlled by the leadership of the majority party, allowing for greater order and efficiency. In the House, a Rules Committee, dominated by the speaker, determines which bills are debated and when. In addition, it determines the rules under which a bill will be passed, for example setting time limits or determining the acceptability of amendments	There is no Rules Committee, which means that the agenda of the Senate is determined by the whole chamber, which has to determine which bills to take up and which to pass over

→

House	Senate
There is virtually no scope for a **filibuster** in the House, with a vote automatically scheduled, usually by the Rules Committee	Bills are subject to a filibuster by an individual senator who can insist that they wish to continue to debate a bill, thus preventing it from being voted on. To overturn a filibuster, a motion of cloture has to be passed, requiring a supermajority to end debate. This effectively means that legislation requires 60 votes to pass the Senate. At the end of Obama's first term, the *Washington Post* listed 17 major bills which would have passed Congress if there was no Senate filibuster, including the DREAM Act on immigration reform, and a repeal of Bush-era tax cuts for millionaires
Unanimous consent can be used in the House but, given the existence of the Rules Committee, it is not commonly exercised. It was used in the first issue to hit the House floor in 2017 after Republicans reduced the power of the Ethics Committee. After a public outcry and critical tweets from President Trump, the House used unanimous consent to quickly restore previous committee protocol	A great deal of use is made of unanimous consent. This involves a proposal being made on the floor of the full Senate, which then only passes if no one objects. It is typically used on procedural issues, helping to determine which bills will be debated, when and under which rules. It is a more unwieldy version of the House Rules Committee. Majority and minority leaders, in consultation with their party caucuses, will attempt to work out a unanimous consent agreement, prescribing a definite time for debate and voting on a bill. In some cases unanimous consent is used to simply pass a bill, such as the passage of the Justice Against Sponsors of Terrorism Act 2016

The policy significance of Congress

Congress can have a major impact on the USA through its policy making. In particular, it can affect:

- social policy, particularly policy on economics, health and education, having a major impact on the daily lives of millions
- political processes such as the voting process, the power of the states and the power of the president

The extent of its impact depends on how successfully Congress can pass laws. The above section covering strengths and weaknesses shows that Congress can be heavily limited in its impact because there are so many obstacles to passing legislation.

Such laws might be highly effective because:

- they are often based on a compromise of different interests — they therefore represent a variety of interests promoting pluralist democracy
- laws are very carefully checked by many different processes in Congress — this series of filters should produce better quality legislation

On the other hand:

- the legislative process is so complex that bills passed may be incoherent, lacking clear direction or containing contradictions in terms of policy goals
- the ability of members of Congress to add amendments, especially benefiting their state, has often led to major increases in federal expenditure, drawing criticisms of money being wasted

Filibuster An individual prevents a vote from taking place by continuing to require time to talk during a debate. This prevents legislation from passing or appointments being ratified because no vote can take place.

Unanimous consent A member of Congress, in the full chamber, may request a vote on a specific procedure for debate in their particular chamber. If no member of that chamber objects then the procedure is adopted.

The effectiveness of these laws is largely a matter of ideological judgement. Liberals are likely to pass negative judgement on much of the laws passed by Republican President Trump and a Republican majority.

An assessment of the impact and effectiveness can be made by applying the ideas above to recent laws or proposals such as:

- the American Recovery and Reinvestment Act signed by Obama, 2009
- the Patient Protection and Affordable Care Act signed by Obama, 2010
- the Omnibus Appropriations Act signed by Trump, May 2017

The impact of Congress is limited by:

- the president, especially the presidential veto
- internal divisions within Congress, making agreement impossible
- partisanship, especially when there is a divided government, making consensus difficult to achieve
- the Supreme Court, which can overturn legislation which is unconstitutional

Oversight

Congressional **oversight** can be carried out through a variety of means such as investigating executive action or providing more concrete checks such as rejecting presidential legislation.

Factors influencing the relationship between Congress and the presidency

The relationship between presidency and Congress is perhaps the most important political relationship in the USA. The extent to which the two institutions can work together has a major impact on the way in which the country is governed. The nature of this relationship can vary a great deal depending on a number of different factors:

- **Party control.** If the president's party holds a majority then the relationship between the two branches is likely to be cooperative. Under **divided government**, a president is likely to face stronger oversight and a competing political agenda. In this sense it could be argued that President Trump worked more cooperatively with Congress in his first 2 years than Obama was able to in his final 6 years.
- **Policy area.** The dual presidency theory suggests that the president is much more constrained in domestic policy than foreign policy. This can be seen with the use of executive agreements or the president initiating military action without congressional consultation as Obama did in Libya in 2011.
- **The popularity of the president.** Presidents can usually wield greater influence when they are at their most popular. Congress is more likely to accede to their wishes out of a desire to maintain popularity. Members of Congress from *both* parties can be affected by this.
- **Partisanship.** The longer term rise in partisanship has had a major effect on presidential-congressional relations, as we shall see later. In short, when the president has a majority there is less resistance to his agenda.

Oversight The ability of one branch of government to scrutinise another branch, including the provision of checks on other branches.

Divided government When the House of Representatives, Senate and presidency are not all controlled by one party.

Checks on the other branches of government

- **Congressional committees.** These committees can investigate executive action or consider legislative proposals, often amending or blocking presidential laws. Congress created the House Select Committee on Benghazi in 2014, after the killing of the US ambassador to Libya. The committee investigated the executive, questioning Hillary Clinton, the Secretary of State at the time of the attack, for over eight hours.
- **Vote on presidential proposals.** This is perhaps the most significant check that Congress places on the presidency, in which it frequently blocks presidential proposals.
- **Ratification of appointments and treaties.** This exclusive power of the Senate can have a major impact on the president's ability to conduct foreign policy and to appoint people who will forward his political agenda. This restriction was particularly acute in 2016 when the Senate refused to vote on Obama's nomination of Merrick Garland to the Supreme Court in 2016, allowing President Trump to influence the ideological balance of the Court by appointing Justice Gorsuch.
- **Impeachment and removal.** While this is the ultimate power of Congress over the president, it can only be used if there is evidence of presidential wrongdoing. President Nixon was not impeached or removed but perhaps the threat of this helped to secure his resignation over the Watergate affair in 1974.

Congress has both the willingness *and* the ability to provide extensive checks as a result of the separation of powers (largely heightening willingness) and checks and balances (affecting ability). On the other hand, the imperial presidency theory suggests that the president often evades the intended constitutional restrictions envisaged by the Founding Fathers. In addition, the rise of executive control over foreign and security policy suggests that Congress is passive in these policy areas, allowing the executive a great deal of control.

> **Knowledge check 15**
>
> How can Congress attempt to provide executive oversight?

Interpretations and debates

The changing powers of Congress

Formal constitutional change accounts for very little of the changes in the power of Congress, perhaps with the exception of the increased democratic legitimacy of the Senate once the 17th Amendment was passed in 1913. A number of other changes have affected congressional power.

- **The growth of the modern presidency.** While this has its roots in earlier presidents, the terms of F. D. Roosevelt can be seen as the beginning of modern presidents who became much more active in developing the legislative agenda of the USA. The growth of the executive office and the rise of national media contributed to a major rebalancing of presidential–congressional relations in which the president then became the chief legislator.
- **Rise in importance of foreign policy.** This has undermined congressional power as international affairs have become increasingly controlled by the presidency. The growth of military technology, the Cold War and the war on terror have all given the president and not Congress the opportunity to take more control of military policy. Congress has attempted to exert authority with the War Powers Act of 1974 but this has sometimes been ignored by presidents.

- **Rise in power of the speaker.** The nationalisation of midterm elections, as well as some changes to congressional procedure, have helped to centralise power in the hands of the House speaker. Under divided government, this has allowed the speaker to act as a significant rival to the president. The speaker is able to lead Congress in providing more effective oversight and develop an alternative policy agenda.
- **Partisanship.** The increased unity of parties has created greater extremes in Congress's reaction to the presidency and the extent to which it has attempted to restrict the executive branch. Under divided government, partisanship has arguably strengthened the power of Congress as it becomes more determined to challenge presidential power.

Debates about the adequacy of its representative role

Representation refers to the extent to which Congress is able to promote the wishes and interests of the people. The importance of many key aspect of Congress covered so far in this chapter can be applied to evaluate the effectiveness of its representative role. Pork-barrel legislation, incumbency, the filibuster, partisanship and gerrymandering all connect to its representative capacity. Congress can be considered highly representative because of:

- the separation of powers and separate mandates from the president
- two elected bodies
- frequent elections and short House terms
- primaries

On the other hand, congressional representation is limited by:

- FPTP, gerrymandering and incumbency
- social representation
- pressure groups
- partisanship

Changing significance of parties in Congress

Parties have become a much more significant force with increased party unity in the form of high levels of partisanship. This rise in partisanship can be seen in the increase in party unity scores, which give a percentage measurement of the extent to which members of the same party vote the same way on each vote. In Congress, the average unity in the 113th Congress (2012–14) was 92% for the Democrats and 90% for Republicans. This figure has steadily increased from the low 70s in the 1970s. There has also been increased polarisation, which has seen the two main parties move ideologically further apart.

The implication of partisanship

- **Legislative gridlock.** The determination to act as a unified group and oppose the other political party has reduced the ability of Congress to pass legislation.
- **Oversight.** The increase in partisanship affects presidential power. Under divided government the president's policy initiatives are aggressively opposed, leaving the president extremely limited. This can be seen in the Obama presidency between 2010 and 2016. Under unified government with one party holding the presidency, House and Senate, congressional politicians have been accused of failing to operate

Exam tip

Partisanship is an important key concept in US politics. It can be applied to all topics. Take time to fully understand the concept and how it relates to each topic.

Exam tip

Many political concepts are complex and you can be rewarded for demonstrating a good understanding of this complexity. Words such as 'representation' can be used without a clear appreciation of what they mean. By applying certain *types* of representation, such as delegates and trustees, you can evaluate with greater depth, perhaps by arguing that Congress is more able to provide one form of representation than another.

their constitutional role in providing oversight and provide significant checks on the executive. In 2017, the Senate was accused of failing to provide full scrutiny of several Trump cabinet nominations given the speed of ratification and the lack of provision of full background checks before votes took place.

■ **Representation.** There is also a debate about the impact this has upon the representative function of Congress, with politicians being accused of sacrificing the needs of voters for party political point scoring.

Significance and effectiveness of constitutional powers

Congress is one of the most powerful legislative bodies in the world. In order to fully understand its power it is essential to understand the provision of both the separation of powers and checks and balances in the Constitution.

Separation of powers ensures:

■ separate elections for president and Congress, giving them both an equal right to govern
■ the possibility of divided government
■ limited presidential patronage power over Congress

Checks and balances allow for significant restrictions on presidential power, using the congressional powers to:

■ reject legislative proposals
■ impeach and remove a president
■ ratify treaties
■ ratify presidential appointments

The significance of these constitutional powers can be evaluated by examining the extent of their influence (see Table 11). Do the powers actually work? How much power do they give to Congress, especially in controlling the president and determining public policy?

> **Knowledge check 16**
>
> Which two constitutional features allow Congress to be such a powerful legislature and how do they do this?

Table 11 The effectiveness of the constitutional powers of Congress

Highly effective	Constitutional power	Limited effectiveness
Congress has a high impact on legislation, initiating, amending and blocking legislation	**To legislate**	The president is highly influential, especially in setting the legislative agenda, limiting congressional impact
Congress has constitutional power here and often limits presidential requests for military action	**To declare war**	Congress is passive in this area, allowing the president a great deal of control over military matters. In addition, presidents sometimes act unilaterally
Amendments have a major impact on the operation of the US political system	**To amend the Constitution**	In practice, amendments are infrequent
Congress has used this power to remove people from office. It is of major importance in checking public officials	**To impeach and remove from office**	While it is theoretically significant, in practice it is not a constant threat, allowing the restriction of presidential power. It is also difficult to achieve

→

Highly effective	Constitutional power	Limited effectiveness
This is of major significance because of the impact treaties have on the USA in both military and economic policy. The Senate has rejected several treaties	**To ratify treaties (Senate)**	The president may use executive agreements to bypass the Senate. Most foreign policy is not conducted through treaties
This power allows the Senate to have a major influence on presidential appointments and therefore the possible policy direction of the USA	**To ratify appointments (Senate)**	Presidents achieve most of their appointments

The extent to which these powers are significant also depends on the factors outlined above under the heading 'Factors influencing the relationship between Congress and the presidency' (page 27).

Comparisons with the UK

Powers, strengths and weaknesses of each of the Houses

Both Parliament and Congress can be seen as similar because:

- they can initiate and amend legislation
- they can determine whether or not a law is passed
- they can vote against executive proposals (especially blocking legislation)
- they can scrutinise the executive

Congress can be considered more powerful than Parliament for these reasons:

- Congress has greater independence from the executive branch than Parliament mainly due to the separation/fusion of powers. This means that Parliament is less willing to challenge the executive.
- Congress has two powerful chambers whereas the Lords in the UK has more limited constitutional powers.
- The US Constitution awards greater powers to Congress to check the executive. The roles of ratifying treaties and declaring war are awarded to Congress in the USA but technically to the prime minister in the UK.

Parliament can be considered more powerful than Congress in these respects:

- Parliamentary sovereignty allows Parliament to make any law it wishes to. Constitutional sovereignty in the USA allows the Supreme Court to overturn Acts of Congress which are unconstitutional.
- The imperial presidency theory suggests that checks and balances are ineffective in the USA, meaning that Parliament is at least as powerful as Congress, if not more so.

The extent to which the Houses are equal

The extent to which the two lower chambers (the House of Representatives and the House of Commons) are equal in power can be assessed by applying many of the points above.

There is a greater contrast between the powers of the Senate and the House of Lords. While the Senate became elected when the Constitution was amended in 1913, the Lords remains unelected. This lack of democratic legitimacy curtails the power of

Knowledge check 17

How does the parliamentary system affect the power of Parliament and how does the presidential system affect the power of Congress?

the Lords. The power of the Senate can also be seen as much greater than that of the Lords, generally for the same reasons that cause Congress to be more powerful than the Commons (see above). In addition:

- the Lords is unable to reject government bills whereas the Senate can prevent presidential policy from passing
- the Lords is not awarded the same powers of executive scrutiny which the Senate is given by the US Constitution (ratification of treaties and appointments)

Rational, cultural and structural approaches

The structural approach is useful in understanding the differences in the power of Congress and Parliament. The structure of the constitution has a huge impact on the powers and limits of Parliament and Congress. The separation of powers and checks and balances are structures which arguably make Congress a significantly more powerful body than Parliament. The fusion of powers in the UK promotes executive dominance of Parliament. The separation of powers in the USA helps to prevent the president dominating Congress.

The cultural approach is more suited to helping understand the role of groups *within* Congress and Parliament. Arguably, parties have a much greater impact in the UK than the USA, with individuals typically working together as a team more than in the USA. This in turn affects the power of Parliament and Congress. Congress may find it less able to pass laws than Parliament because of the lack of party unity. A stronger party culture might make Congress more effective, allowing for more agreement to be reached by the majority party.

The rational approach allows students to understand the self-interested motivations of legislative politicians. In both Parliament and Congress, politicians are acting in a self-interested manner because they will act to ensure their own political careers through re-election. This may lead politicians to ignore *the structures* of the executive and party leaders or *the cultural expectation* of party membership in order to respond to public opinion and gain re-election.

Summary

- Congress is a bicameral legislature with two chambers having different features.
- While both chambers are co-equal legislative bodies, there are exclusive powers for each chamber.
- Congress has three main functions: to legislate, to represent and to check (oversight).
- High incumbency re-election rates are a major feature of Congress.
- Members of Congress are influenced by their party, their constituency and pressure groups.
- The legislative process is a complex one in which it is difficult to pass legislation.
- Congress is a powerful legislative body due to the separation of powers and powers awarded to it by the Constitution.
- Congress has both representative strengths and weaknesses.
- Congress can check the president, often limiting his power significantly.
- Although there are many factors which affect the relationship between president and Congress, the key ones are the four Ps of party control, policy area, popularity and partisanship.
- The role and power of Congress have changed over time, especially with the rise of presidential power.
- The role of parties has changed in recent years with the rise in partisanship.

■ US presidency

Formal sources of presidential powers and their use

There are a number of enumerated powers given to the president in the Constitution — this is the key formal source of his power and does not vary between presidents or throughout their term in office. It is important to note that the Constitution gives 'executive power' to 'a President' — the singular nature of this means that all the other parts of the **executive branch** have limited, or no, constitutional power.

The enumerated powers of the president are as follows:

- Execute laws faithfully
- Power of pardon
- Veto or sign legislation
- Commander-in-chief
- State of the Union address
- Make treaties
- Appointments of federal justices and cabinet officers
- Request opinions of the heads of executive departments
- Recess appointments
- Receive ambassadors
- Convene or adjourn both Houses on extraordinary occasions

While these powers do not vary in theory, the ability of a president to exercise these powers effectively does depend on a range of factors including his popularity, control over Congress and time in office. These are outlined in the section on 'Informal sources', pages 36–39. It is notable that many of these powers are proactive — they allow the president to act first and then ask for congressional approval. Comparatively, many of Congress's powers are reactive — they require the president to bring something to Congress before it can act.

Professor Neustadt argued that these enumerated powers do not actually give the president much power on their own — rather that it is in the president's personal ability and resources that the true power lies. Nonetheless, these powers give the president a considerable foundation for his authority.

The roles of head of state and head of government

Head of state

The role of head of state encompasses a number of functions:

- Military — in dealing with foreign affairs as commander-in-chief
- Judicial — in exercising the power of the pardon
- Diplomatic — in receiving ambassadors and making treaties
- Ceremonial — in undertaking expected public tasks and duties

Executive branch As a theoretical branch of government, this is the one which executes, or carries out, law. In the USA, this is the presidency and consists of the president, vice-president, EXOP, cabinet and the federal bureaucracy.

Knowledge check 18

What are implied powers of the president?

Exam tip

Students often see these powers as effective or ineffective based on their use. Sometimes *not* using them can also show strength, for example the threat of the veto or the lack of need to use the veto due to controlling both Houses of Congress. As always, looking at context is key.

■ Legislative — in giving the State of the Union address, which has become a list of legislative expectations from the president

■ Representative of the USA — in meeting world leaders, attending summits or responding to national disasters/tragedies

As head of state, many of these roles do not come from enumerated powers given within the Constitution, but from the expected tasks of the president. This means that many of them have few checks outlined in the Constitution. Table 12 lists the various roles and the checks on them, along with recent examples from Obama's presidency.

Knowledge check 19

Of what does the US Constitution say that the president is the commander-in-chief?

Table 12 Roles of the president as head of state and checks upon these

Role	Example	Constitutional checks*
Military	Obama and air strikes on Libya and Syria	Theoretically, power to declare war, but not used since 1941
Judicial	Obama commuted sentences for 330 people on his last day in office, many for 'mandatory minimum' offences	None
Diplomatic	Obama began talks, and wrote to President Castro, to begin 'normalising' relations between Cuba and the USA in 2014	Treaties must be confirmed by Senate, but not executive orders or agreements Congress does not have the power to approve ambassadors *to* the USA, only *from* the USA
Ceremonial	Traditionally, a president pardons a turkey on Thanksgiving and throws a ceremonial first pitch in baseball, as Obama did in 2010	None
Legislative	At Obama's 2016 State of the Union address, he left an empty chair in his number of invites, signifying Congress's failure to achieve meaningful legislation on gun control	There are no real checks on the State of the Union speech itself — a president is free to say what he pleases. The impact of this speech, however, is dependent on Congress's power to write and amend legislation
Representative	Obama attended the Paris Climate Change Conference in 2016 and brokered the Iran nuclear deal as a 'non-binding agreement' in 2015 Obama addressed the nation after the Oregon shooting in 2015	None

* Congress does have the power to sign the budget and to 'investigate', both of which could be used to try and check any of these roles; the effectiveness, however, is questionable given that investigations occur only after an event and the president writes the budget.

Most of these roles are beyond the borders of the USA, which explains the limited nature of checks.

Head of government

As head of government, the president carries out functions which are more domestic in nature:

- Executive — in executing laws of Congress using the federal bureaucracy and appointing cabinet members and federal justices
- Legislative — in delivering a legislative programme at the State of the Union address and signing or vetoing legislation that is put forward from Congress
- Military — in protecting the individual states. Constitutionally, this refers to civil war between states but today is more likely to mean responding to natural disasters or acts of terrorism.

Table 13 lists the above roles and the checks on them, along with recent examples.

Table 13 Roles of the president as head of government and checks upon these

Role	Example	Constitutional checks*
Executive	Obama appointed two Supreme Court justices — Sotomayor and Kagan	Appointments need to be ratified by the Senate
	Trump nominated Gorsuch	If Congress uses a veto override, as with Obama's 9/11 Victims Bill, the president must carry out this law
Legislative	Obama suggested a minimum wage law in his 2015 State of the Union address	Congress can use the veto override
	Obama vetoed 12 pieces of legislation from Congress	Congress must introduce and pass all legislation before the president chooses to sign or veto it
Military	Bush sent in troops to help restore order after Hurricane Katrina in 2005	None explicitly, but states' powers are protected through federalism and subsequent laws mean the president can only deploy troops within the USA with permission of the individual state or to protect constitutional rights
	Obama sent 1,000 National Guardsmen to the US–Mexico border in 2010	

* Congress does have the power to sign the Budget and to 'investigate', both of which could be used to try and check any of these roles; the effectiveness, however, is questionable given that investigations occur only after an event and the president writes the Budget.

The role of head of government has far more checks on it as Congress's primary concern is **domestic politics**. It may often be, therefore, that a president relies more on his role of head of state as his presidency continues, as it is likely that his approval rating will decline across his presidency.

Exam tip

As with so many comparisons, you should not see the line between head of state and head of government as distinct — the Constitution does not use these terms. However, in exams, a good rule of thumb is that head of state largely deals with foreign policy and has fewer checks, whereas head of government deals with domestic policy and has more checks.

Knowledge check 20

Name one natural disaster and one national event that a president since 1992 has responded to by using the military.

Domestic politics The policies that affect the running of a country *within* the borders of that country and that directly affect the lives of citizens, for example healthcare, gun control, racial issues — in contrast to foreign policy.

Informal sources of presidential powers and their use

The electoral mandate, executive orders, national events and the cabinet

Electoral mandate

One way in which a president can remain powerful is through the mandate he received from the public during an election. Such powers, not derived from the Constitution, can be described as **informal powers.**

> ### Exam tip
>
> Always relate informal powers back to an individual president and how he can use them to gain power, or how his own actions work to limit his power.

Table 14 Presidential election results (a selection)

Year	Party	President	Popular vote	% popular vote	Electoral College
1992	Democratic	Clinton	44,909,806	43.0	370 / 538
2000	Republican	Bush	50,456,002	47.9	271 / 538
2008	Democratic	Obama	69,498,516	52.9	365 / 538
2016	Republican	Trump	62,979,636	46.0	304 / 538

Each of the elections listed in Table 14 is interesting — in 1992 Clinton won a plurality but not a majority due to the success of Ross Perot taking 19% of the national vote. In 2000 and 2016, both Bush and Trump won in the Electoral College but not the popular vote. In 2008, Obama won a clear majority, a landslide by Democrat standards. 2008 and 2016 make particularly useful comparisons. While Obamacare was controversial, with a popular **electoral mandate** and support in both Houses, Obama was able to get it passed. Despite Trump taking both Houses too, he has been hampered with problems from the outset due in part to his unprecedented lack of popularity, gaining the fastest majority disapproval rating of any US president.

Executive orders

Executive orders are not as suspicious as they are often portrayed — for the most part, they are simply a directive from the president to his cabinet departments on how he would like law to be carried out. However, a president can use this as a form of **unilateral action** to achieve a policy goal that he may be struggling to complete elsewhere.

Famously, Nixon created the Environmental Protection Agency with an executive order. However, these orders can be overturned by the Supreme Court or by a new law of Congress. Obama ordered Guantanamo Bay to be closed as well as DAPA (Deferred Action for Parents of Americans) and DACA (Deferred Action for Childhood Arrivals) to be expanded; Guantanamo remains open and his DAPA/DACA order was overturned by the Supreme Court in 2016. He also used an

Informal powers Powers of the president, or ways in which the president can be powerful, that are not listed in the Constitution.

Electoral mandate An electoral mandate is the permission granted to a political leader or winning party to govern and act on the people's behalf, for example to President Obama in 2008 and 2012.

Knowledge check 21

How did George W. Bush and Trump manage to win the presidency despite not winning the popular vote?

Executive orders A direction to the federal bureaucracy on how the president would like a piece of legislation to be implemented.

executive order to extend background checks for gun purchase, which remained in place until the newly-elected Republican Congress overturned it in 2017. His order giving federal employees a minimum wage of $10.10 was perhaps more successful.

National events

A president can use a national event to gain an advantage in trying to achieve policy goals. Obama was able to utilise national tragedies such as the Sandy Hook and Orlando shootings to press for greater gun control in the USA, or the Gulf of Mexico oil spill to advance his green agenda. That 9/11 happened in 2001 helped George Bush to become more presidential after the controversy that surrounded his election. However, such events, if poorly managed, can backfire too. The wars in Iraq and Afghanistan ultimately cost Bush a great deal of power once they became unpopular with the American people and resulted in him losing control of Congress. Equally, his slow response to Hurricane Katrina led to some claiming this was due to racism (due to the disproportionate number of minorities affected) — the truth of this was almost unimportant when compared to the headlines.

The cabinet

The cabinet has existed since 1793 and is formed today of the heads of the 15 departments of government, plus others that the president wishes to include. Obama included the head of the Environmental Protection Agency, the head of the Council of Economic Advisors, the UN ambassador and the US trade representative — all of these speak to his personal beliefs or the key issues he was facing in his presidency.

As a source of power, the cabinet is used to show open, transparent government. The Obama administration created one of the most diverse cabinets in history to give a vast range of voters a feeling of inclusion within government. This would hopefully improve presidential approval. Equally, the cabinet can give the president a source of power in its expertise.

However, traditionally, the cabinet is seen as a poor and unreliable source of presidential power, because.

- it has no constitutional power
- the cabinet is not a collective body
- its members are based away from the White House in their departments, as opposed to in EXOP

Exam tip

You should have a couple of detailed case studies of cabinet members and their impact — just naming a cabinet member is not enough.

Individually, a cabinet member may be incredibly useful to the president, either in being the force behind one of his policies, as with Sebelius and Obamacare, or in taking some of the criticism away from the president himself, such as Sebelius, rather than Obama, being the named defendant when Obamacare came to the Supreme Court. Equally, when a cabinet member publicly criticises the president, such as Chuck Hagel (Secretary of Defense) over Guantanamo detainees being released, this can damage the president's power.

Unilateral action An action by the president in which he attempts to make a decision alone, without the input or consultation of Congress.

Exam tip

Make sure you know the definition of executive orders, in particular that they are not new laws. Also, ensure you are clear that, because they are simply directives on how a law is to be enforced, Congress can effectively overrule executive orders by changing the law.

Knowledge check 22

Why is the US cabinet not a collective body?

Powers of persuasion, including the nature/characteristics of each president

Professor Neustadt's often quoted line is that 'presidential power is the power to persuade'. With a lack of patronage, no direct control over Congress and a weak party system, it can be difficult for the president to get what he wants, hence this claim.

Nature/characteristics of each president

Table 15 The circumstances of four recent presidents

President	House control	Senate control	Key national events	Approval ratings
Clinton (Democrat)	Democrat 1993–95 Republican 1995–2001	Democrat 1993–95 Republican 1995–2001	Oklahoma bombing Lewinsky scandal Government shutdown 1995–96	Highest 73% Lowest 37%
Bush (Republican)	Republican 2001–07 Democrat 2007–09	Democrat 2001–03 Republican 2003–07 Democrat 2007–09	9/11 and subsequent wars Hurricane Katrina Economic crash	Highest 90% Lowest 25%
Obama (Democrat)	Democrat 2009-2011 Republican 2011–17	Democrat 2009–15 Republican 2015–17	Mass shootings — Sandy Hook, Orlando, Oregon, etc. Osama Bin Laden killed Benghazi Government shutdown 2013	Highest 68% Lowest 40%
Trump (Republican)	Republican 2017–19	Republican 2017–19	'Muslim travel ban' executive order	Highest 46% Lowest 38%

Exam tip

One of the most common questions students ask is 'How old can my examples be?' The best answer is 'When did it last happen?' Always aim for the most recent example of whatever you are discussing — if you were talking about the Vietnam War, the examiner would wonder why you were not talking about Syria.

Powers of persuasion This is an informal power of the president in which he can use the prestige of the job and other bargaining methods in order to get people to do as he wishes.

There have been examples where a president has had to resort to **powers of persuasion** to get his way — Clinton telephoned Margolies-Mezvinsky in 1993 to get her all-important vote to secure his budget; Obama, frustrated by Congress, claimed he had a 'pen and a phone' and would get things done that way.

The personality of each president, coupled with the factors in Table 15, explain their effectiveness in 'persuasion'. Clinton was well liked, despite the scandal, and managed to achieve a lot despite an opposition Congress — his experience of governor of a right-leaning state helped him in working with Republicans. By contrast, Bush was able to get lots done under the guise of the 'war on terror', which dominated so much of his presidency. Comparatively, Obama was often characterised by his cool, calm and collected nature, which made him seem aloof in some circumstances. Instead he relied on his vice-president, with decades of Senate experience and contacts, to get the minutiae of policy carried out.

Nonetheless, often the power of persuasion relies on having real constitutional power to back it up, or an ability to rely on unilateral action if this does not work.

The Executive Office of the President (EXOP)

EXOP was established in 1939 following the Brownlow Committee Report that found 'the president needs help'. EXOP consists of approximately 1,500–2,000 people, directly accountable to the president, of which a good number operate directly out of the White House — the 'west wing'. They are an important source of presidential power as they are his most trusted advisors; when they speak, they speak on behalf of the president.

National Security Council (NSC)

The NSC consists of a wide array of security staff — the president and vice-president, heads of State and Defense, as well as the chairman of the Joint Chiefs of Staff, the CIA, the National Security Advisor (NSA) and others. Their role, however, has been hugely dependent on the president. Both Nixon and George W. Bush used the NSC and the NSA in favour of the State Department, and under Reagan it was the NSAs who ran the Iran–Contra affair. All of this can court negative publicity for the president, which can ultimately have a limiting effect on his power. Comparatively, in the famous picture of Obama watching Osama bin Laden being captured, he is surrounded by his NSC; for a president with limited foreign policy or military experience this afforded him considerable gravitas.

Office of Management and Budget (OMB)

The OMB is responsible for handling the budget that the president presents to Congress, and for monitoring what each department is spending. Given that this role allows the OMB considerable power, its director was made a Senate-confirmable appointment. According to the White House Transition Project:

> OMB's knowledge and expertise strengthens the president's hand in dealings with the Congress during the annual budget process. OMB communicates with Congress at many levels through numerous channels. At the top, those Directors who were armed by mastery of numbers and policy details became the president's most effective representative and advocate in negotiations with congressional leaders. At lower levels, OMB staff have usually been available to their counterparts on the Hill to provide technical explanation and analysis of the president's proposals and other policy ideas.

White House Office (WHO)

Led by the president's chief of staff, members of the WHO advise the president by assessing the advice he has been sent by others, and reviewing recommendations, for example by cabinet officers. The best-recognised face in this office is usually the press secretary — for Trump, Sean Spicer was the source of ridicule in the press due to the administration's antagonistic relationship with the media. This has cost Trump a good deal of 'power' in the way he and his administration have been reported on. For Obama, special advisors such as David Axelrod were trusted to speak to the press without asking Obama first, such as when Axelrod defended Sotomayor following her confirmation controversy. Such personal, trusted staff can be an asset to presidential power, but are dangerously close to the president if they court negative public attention.

Exam tip

EXOP can be difficult to find detailed examples for, given the 'closed door' nature of its operation. Documentaries such as the BBC's 2016 *Inside Obama's White House* do offer lots of these examples, however.

Knowledge check 23

What constitutional power does EXOP have?

The presidency

Relationship between the presidency and Congress, and why this varies

The key factor that determines the president's relationship with Congress is the party in control of either House. While controlling one or both Houses does not guarantee a president success in legislation, it is certainly beneficial. Both Bush and Obama relied far more heavily on the veto once they lost control of Congress — Bush using all 11 of his vetoes in his last 2 years, and Obama using 10 of 12 vetoes in the same period. Both presidents also found it harder to push through their legislative agenda once they lost control, and instead used other, unilateral, powers such as executive orders to try and circumvent this problem.

Presidential approval, as well as time in office, is a key factor affecting their relationship with Congress. Congress is often much more willing to challenge the president if his approval ratings are lower. Bush struggling to deal with the financial crisis in 2008 and Obama's immigration and gun control failures illustrate this.

National events also affect this relationship — in times of national emergency, Congress often acts with deference to the president, allowing him greater freedom to act and respond as he pleases. This was evident in its 'blank cheque' to Bush given 48 hours after the 9/11 attack.

Knowledge check 24

When did both G. W. Bush and Obama lose complete control of Congress?

Relationship between the presidency and the Supreme Court, and why this varies

The president has limited influence over the Supreme Court. If he is fortunate enough to be able to fill a vacancy, he can by no means guarantee his nominee will get ratified, or if they do, that they will decide in a manner the president would agree with. However, in these circumstances the president can attempt to alter the ideological balance of the Supreme Court, such as when Bush replaced centrist Day O'Connor with conservative Alito, effectively swinging the Court to a conservative majority.

The president's support of Supreme Court decisions can affect the relationship. Bush effectively found himself being challenged in the Court three times in 5 years over Guantanamo Bay, once as a named defendant. Each time, the effect of the ruling was limited due to Bush's support of Guantanamo Bay. Obama openly criticised the Court's decision in *Citizens United* v *FEC*, saying they had 'opened the floodgates' on corporations influencing elections, and yet his criticism achieved little to negate the impact of the ruling.

Equally, the decisions the Court takes on the president can affect both his power and their relationship. Obama found himself positively involved in *Sebelius* v *NFIB* which upheld Obamacare, but then in 2016 the Court struck down his immigration executive orders in *Texas* v *US*. The latter of these was particularly damaging, leaving the first minority president with negligible progress to show on immigration reform.

Exam tip

Understanding and addressing the phrase 'varies' is crucial to gaining top marks. Note that each president may gain or lose power against the other two branches at various times and for various reasons.

Limitations on presidential power and why this varies between presidents

The changing nature of power over a president's term in office

The power of any president is not fixed — it fluctuates over time depending on many of the factors listed above. Usually, the power of a president can be compared to that of Congress if 'power' is imagined as a bar chart, as shown in Table 16:

Table 16 The changing nature of power during a presidency

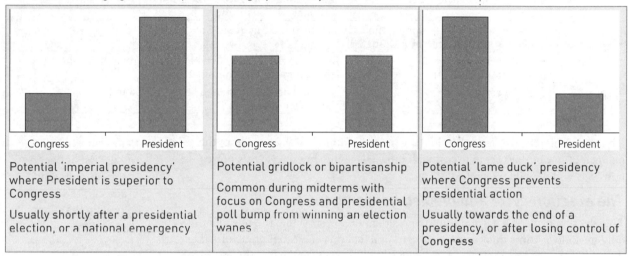

Potential 'imperial presidency' where President is superior to Congress	Potential gridlock or bipartisanship	Potential 'lame duck' presidency where Congress prevents presidential action
Usually shortly after a presidential election, or a national emergency	Common during midterms with focus on Congress and presidential poll bump from winning an election wanes	Usually towards the end of a presidency, or after losing control of Congress

Of course, this is not fixed for every president. Events are key when looking at the changing power of a president: Obama experienced an unexpected bump in power at the very end of his presidency and following a difficult 2016, as the election of Trump had the effect of gaining him popularity. Key factors that change over the course of a presidency and affect the president's power could be:

- electoral mandate
- national events and emergencies
- control of Congress
- when the next election is due

Congress, the Supreme Court and the Constitution

Separation of powers and checks and balances ensure that there are a number of constitutional limitations on the president, as well as further informal checks placed on the president. As the US Constitution is codified, and therefore judiciable, if a president ignores these limitations he can find himself being held accountable in the Supreme Court. However, the key here is again the nature of these powers — in almost all cases, especially when looking at constitutional checks, the president is required to act (proactive) before he can be checked by either branch (reactive). This is shown in Table 17.

There are some cases in which Congress can act first; it could write any legislation it sees fit, especially if under control of a different party to the president. However, not only does the president have the veto, he also controls the federal bureaucracy, whose

Exam tip

Remember, all these theories (see Table 16) are simply observations by political scientists of what is going on in politics and therefore can be wrong or change — do not be worried if you can find exceptions to these theories in your studies.

Knowledge check 25

Who first wrote about the 'imperial presidency' and why?

Table 17 Actions needed by the president before Congress or the Supreme Court can act

Branch	Power	What the president must do first
Congress	Delay, amend, pass or reject legislation (Article I, Section 1)	Suggest legislation at the State of the Union address
		Can threaten to veto in order to force change before it gets to him for signature
	Ratify treaties and appointments (Article II, Section 2, Clause 2)	Nominate appointees and put forward written treaties Can end treaties without congressional consent
	Declare war (Article I, Section 8, Clause 11)	Can move troops; War Powers Act 1973 ineffective (and arguably unconstitutional)
	Power of the purse — signing the Budget (Article I, Section 7, Clause 9)	Suggest the Budget to Congress
	Filibustering and senatorial holds (unanimous consent)	As these are usually used to stop nominees advancing, these come after a nomination
Supreme Court	Judicial review	Commit an act which has been argued to be 'unconstitutional'

job it is to enforce such laws. While there are many limits on the president, the balance of power does seem to rest with him. His ability to exercise this power however, will depend on context.

The election cycle and divided government

The election cycle is a natural limit to presidential power. While the president is only formally a 'lame duck' for 6 weeks, in practice this can extend much further depending on when a president loses control of Congress, and when the invisible primary for the next presidential election begins, especially if the incumbent cannot run in it due to term limits. Divided government can be a particular cause of this. A situation with two different parties controlling a branch each, and each branch having constitutional powers, can lead to congressional domination if the president is seen as outgoing and Congress has a fresher mandate. Obama's last 2 years show a mixed picture of power (see Table 18), with the Democrats having lost Congress and with the invisible primary for the 2016 election beginning 18 months before the election.

Table 18 Selected successes and failures from Obama's final 2 years in office

Successes	Failures
Iran nuclear deal struck	DAPA/DACA struck down by Supreme Court
Ten vetoes cast; nine of which stood, including Keystone Pipeline	Merrick Garland denied nomination hearing
Executive orders used to close gun background check loopholes	9/11 Victims Bill veto overridden
330 commutations on final day in office	Failure to achieve meaningful gun control or immigration reform legislation
Paris climate change deal agreed to	2017 Budget passed with language which could allow for the repeal of Obamacare

Lame duck Officially the period between the election taking place and the winner taking up that post (November–January). Unofficially, used to refer to a president who seems to lack the power and ability to pass his legislative and policy agenda.

Exam tip

Context is everything. The theory of US politics underpins the study, but how this works in reality always depends on the situation. You must be able to show where presidents with the same power and limitations have had different outcomes due to the circumstances of their presidency.

Interpretations and debates of the US presidency

How effectively they have achieved their aims

In order to assess the effectiveness of achieving their aims, it is crucial to have an understanding of the policy platform of each president. Table 19 gives details of some of the promises and achievements of Clinton, Bush and Obama.

Knowledge check 26

Annually, where do presidents set out their aims?

Table 19 Selected achievements of US presidents since 1992

President	Promises	Achievements
Clinton 1993–2001 'The era of big government is over'	■ Reduce budget deficit and federal bureaucracy size ■ Waiting period on handguns ■ Healthcare reform ■ Promises regarding equal civil rights for all ■ Improvement in education standardisation ■ Responsibility for the environment	■ Achieved a 50% cut in the budget deficit ■ Brady Bill passed ■ 'Hillarycare' failed to gain support and pass Congress ■ Passed Don't Ask Don't Tell, but also signed the Defense of Marriage Act ■ Goals 2000 Program gave billions to schools but the results were largely down to states and therefore not uniform ■ Millions of acres of federal forests and land placed under protection or declared national monuments
Bush 2001–09 'Compassionate conservatism'	■ Tax cuts, especially for lowest earners ■ Social security and Medicare reform ■ Commitment to public education ■ War on terror	■ Trillions of tax cuts delivered but the top 20% of earners benefited most, and a following recession meant this led to a widening deficit ■ Huge Medicare reform in 2003 ■ No Child Left Behind Act signed ■ Both of these policies came at huge expense, with government spending up 33% ■ PATRIOT Act passed, Guantanamo Bay opened and troops put into Afghanistan and Iraq — all eventually at huge cost to his popularity
Obama 2009–17 'Change we can believe in'	■ Close Guantanamo Bay ■ Universal healthcare ■ Mandatory minimum reform ■ End war in Iraq and Afghanistan ■ Equality of pay ■ Immigration reform ■ Gun control	■ Guantanamo Bay executive order and release of detainees, but it remains open ■ Obamacare passed ■ Fair Sentencing Act and Sentencing Reform and Corrections Act passed, but disparities remain ■ 2010 saw the end to Iraq, but Afghanistan drawdown has been more difficult ■ Lilly Ledbetter Act signed but a woman's pay is still only 79% of a man's ■ DREAM Act, DAPA/DACA all largely failed or struck down ■ Relied on executive orders for gun control, failing to get congressional action

The imperial presidency

This is effectively a debate over the power that a president can exert during his time in office — the key focus must be the powers that he has and whether he can exercise them, and the extent to which checks and balances work to limit the president, all of which is highlighted above.

Imperial presidency A dominant presidency with ineffective checks and balances from the other branches.

The important distinction to make here is that a president is rarely identified as *just imperial* or *imperilled* — usually this fluctuates across the course of his presidency. Equally, a president may be imperial in one sphere, for example foreign policy, while being imperilled in another, for example domestic policy.

> **Exam tip**
>
> Ensure that you focus on the difference between foreign and domestic policy here, and look at both enumerated and inherent powers. An imperial president is more likely to rely on poorly checked powers such as the veto, pardon and executive orders.

The extent of presidential accountability to Congress

The ways in which a president is accountable *to* Congress are dealt with above. How far a president can be held to account *by* Congress will be determined by a range of factors:

- **Which party controls Congress.** A president is far less likely to get his legislative agenda passed during divided government; scrutiny is much lower during times of **unified government**, for example Obama and failure on immigration reform.
- **Willingness to use 'imperial' powers such as the veto.** Both Bush and Obama relied heavily on the veto in their last 2 years, compared to none for Bush and only two for Obama in their first 6 years.
- **Circumstances.** Congress is only able to hold the president accountable if it has something he wants. Obama failed to get Garland confirmed but was only able to nominate him due to an unexpected Supreme Court vacancy.

The role and power of the president in foreign policy

The president has a number of key foreign policy powers, mostly exercised as head of state:

- Writing and agreeing treaties
- Receiving ambassadors, and therefore recognising countries
- Commander-in-chief
- Use of executive agreements
- Meeting world leaders, attending summits (e.g. G7/8).
- Control over instruments of foreign policy such as the State Department, the Defense Department and the NSC

In this sphere, most of the president's power is poorly checked by Congress; the Founding Fathers left the president enough room to manoeuvre in this area because, according to Ford, 'our forefathers knew you couldn't have 535 Commanders in Chief and Secretaries of State. It just wouldn't work'. Often, internationally, the USA needs to be seen to speak and act with one voice, and that is the role of the president. However, that is not to say Congress does not control him.

- **AUMF (Authorisation for the Use of Military Force).** While war has not been formally declared since 1941, the use of AUMF is reasonably commonplace and denied Obama the right to intervene in Syria in 2013.

Imperilled presidency
This is the contrasting theory to that of an imperial presidency — it is claimed that the president does not have enough power to be effective.

> **Exam tip**
>
> Be wary of demonstrating that a president is imperilled as he was 'beaten' by Congress — if he can find a way around this, like Obama and DAPA/DACA, then he is not imperilled.

Unified government
Where both Houses of Congress and the presidency are controlled by people from the same political party.

Knowledge check 27
Why may the Founding Fathers have given the president more freedom to act in foreign policy?

- **Power of the purse.** In 2007, the Democrats attempted to use this power to defund the Iraq War.
- **Power to ratify cabinet officials.** Bush's nomination (and recess appointment) of UN-critic John Bolton to the post of US Ambassador to the UN drew so much criticism from Congress he stood down. Three Obama nominees were withdrawn due to various allegations, such as Daschle's unpaid $140,000 tax. John Tower was unsuccessful in his 1989 nomination to defense secretary due to excessive womanising and drinking.

> **Exam tip**
>
> Do not confuse the lack of use of a power with that power being useless. Often the threat of a power being exercised can be far more useful. For example, Harriet Miers withdrew, as did Bolton, knowing they were unlikely to get confirmed by Senate. This is arguably the power being effective. Impeachment and the veto are exactly the same.

Comparisons with the UK

The role and powers of the US president and UK prime minister

Similarities

- Both of these executives depend greatly on charisma and personality to succeed — the 'power to persuade'.
- Both are responsible for extensive appointments within their executive branch — the power of patronage.
- Both assume the role of commander-in-chief in reality, even if the monarch is the head of the UK armed forces in theory.
- Both represent their country on an international stage and in effect control foreign policy.
- Both see their power fluctuate depending on the extent of control over the legislature and circumstances.

Differences

- The UK prime minister is only the head of government and not head of state; whereas the president can enact laws, the prime minister needs the formal assent of the monarch to do so.
- The president has a direct mandate from the people, whereas the prime minister holds power only by virtue of heading the main party.
- The UK prime minister heads the executive, but cabinet is collective and can cost a PM his or her job. The president *is* the executive, and cabinet is merely an advisory body he can use as he pleases.
- The president is bound by a written constitution which limits his power and has structures within it which allow for his removal. The PM can be removed by Parliament but with majority support this is unlikely; the unwritten constitution gives the PM a lot of flexibility in terms of power.

> **Exam tip**
>
> It is worth knowing which prime ministers and presidents were in charge at the same time, as international circumstances will have been the same for them both and this makes it easier for you to compare their responses.

- The UK is a unitary state, giving the PM extensive power across the whole of the country, whereas the US president shares sovereignty not only with other branches of government, but also with the states.

Their impact on politics and government

- **Legislative.** Both the PM and the president effectively lead the legislative programmes for their country, thereby having a huge impact on public policy. However, the UK prime minister is more able to control the content of legislation due to Parliament's unitary power and the PM's majority control; the president may find he has to compromise in order to get his legislation through.
- **Government.** The UK prime minister is the head of a government of fused powers, effectively enabling the PM to control the executive and the legislature, while the Supreme Court has no constitutional sovereign power. This gives prime ministers extensive control over the people they choose to be in government. The US president has perhaps greater control over the people in government, appointing cabinet members and Supreme Court justices, but has limited influence over them and Congress once they are in.
- **Parties.** While the president is often viewed as the head of his party, he is not; the leader of the Republican National Committee currently is not Trump but Priebus, who is responsible for developing party platforms. The prime minister by contrast does head the party, and with extensive powers of patronage is able to control the policy production far more closely.

The extent of accountability to the US and UK legislatures

- **Legislative.** The US president is utterly dependent on Congress for the passing of his legislative programme, which he may not control. Except in rare circumstances, the UK prime minister controls a majority in the House of Commons, allowing the PM to pass legislation with limited scrutiny.
- **Foreign policy.** The US president and the UK prime minister have extensive freedom to act in foreign policy on behalf of the country. However, the US president is more likely to find himself challenged when he loses control of Congress, for example Obama and Iran, Syria and Afghanistan. While UK prime ministers may be challenged, they are more likely to get their way.
- **Second chambers.** The US president has to be concerned not only with the actions of one House, but two. The Senate also has the use of the filibuster and senatorial holds to thwart his wishes. The UK House of Lords, while increasingly bellicose, is less able to thwart the prime minister due to the Salisbury Convention and the unelected nature of the Lords.

Rational, cultural and structural approaches

Many of the actions of both the president and the prime minister can be seen in a rational, selfish sense. This may be either actions to protect their positions of power or actions to enact policy which they are personally in favour of. Obama fought for a change to mandatory minimums consistently, using both legislative power and executive power to do so, while Cameron pushed through the legalisation of same-sex marriage despite claims it could cost him his position.

> **Exam tip**
>
> Always make sure you use the word 'rational', 'cultural' or 'structural' in your Section B answers — do not leave your examiner in any doubt!

However, the impact of cultural theory, especially the roles of parties with shared beliefs, is crucial too. Prime ministers have to act in a way that is in line with their party rather than personal belief, not only because they are the head but because they depend on their party's support in Parliament. It can be seen that this was the reason Cameron allowed a referendum on Brexit, as many in his party shared this belief. Equally, the president being aligned to one party means that many of his policies share this ideology. It would be arbitrary to see a clear distinction between rational and cultural here as most politicians join the party with which they *personally* have a *shared belief.*

Structural theory is crucial to understanding the extent of power and how this may affect an executive's actions. It would be fruitless for a president to threaten a veto if he knew it could be overridden, as this is likely to make him look weak. Therefore, many of the president's decisions would need to be weighed against the likelihood of checks and balances being effective. Comparatively, the UK party structure, which includes very powerful whips, allows the opposite outcome for a prime minister — this structure, coupled with fused powers, allows at times almost complete domination of the UK political landscape with little need for consideration of compromise.

Summary

- The US president is granted extensive powers in the Constitution from Article II, which is far more vague, and therefore flexible, than Article I.
- The balance of power seems to rest with the president, his powers being far more proactive than those granted to Congress.
- The president is a singular executive — all the supporting institutions of this branch have no constitutional power, although may have considerable power in reality.
- The extent of power of the president is determined not by the Constitution alone, but by a wide range of concurrent factors including the timing of the election cycle, the president's personality and charisma, the control of Congress and national circumstances, the year of his presidency — the 'context' of the presidency.
- The president operates in differing spheres of power as head of state and head of government. The head of state role, dealing largely with foreign policy, is considerably less well checked than the head of government role, which deals largely with domestic policy.
- The use of powers granted to the president is not the only measure of his power. There are powers that are important but not enumerated, such as the use of executive orders, but also the threat of using some of these powers (the veto, for example) is enough to force the change that the president wants without actually using them formally.

■ US Supreme Court and civil rights

The nature and role of the Supreme Court

The US Supreme Court was referred to by Alexander Hamilton, one of the Founding Fathers, as the 'least dangerous branch of government':

> The judiciary...has no influence over either the sword or the purse; no direction either of the strength or of the wealth of the society; and can take no active resolution whatever. It may truly be said to have neither FORCE nor WILL, but merely judgment; and must ultimately depend upon the aid of the executive arm even for the efficacy of its judgments.
>
> Alexander Hamilton, *The Federalist Papers*, No. 78

The US Constitution

The Supreme Court is outlined in Article III of the US Constitution in just 377 words; this is compared to 2,267 words for Congress in Article I and 1,025 for the president in Article II. It is a vague article that gives little in the way of explicit power.

'**Judicial review**' is often cited as one of the principles of the Constitution. While this is commonly accepted, it was not until later cases (see page 49) that the Supreme Court actually took this power, meaning its role as constitutionally stated is in fact very limited.

What does Article III state?

- 'Judicial power' is vested in the Supreme Court.
- Congress can establish courts.
- Justices have life tenure in their job in times of 'good behaviour' and their salary is protected.
- The Supreme Court is an **appellate court**, except for in limited circumstances in which it has '**original jurisdiction**'.
- Section 2 outlines all the types of cases the Court can hear, for example cases involving the USA, between two states and between a citizen and a state, and limits its power to hearing cases which arise 'under this Constitution'.

Beyond these key points, there is little said of the Court's power. However, the final point is crucial — in allowing the Supreme Court to review only cases which come from the Constitution, this allows the Court to be the only body which interprets the Constitution, and to some extent lends it sovereignty in that it is interpreting the sovereign document.

The independent nature of the Supreme Court

The independence of the Supreme Court is guaranteed constitutionally and through other processes surrounding the Court.

Judicial review The ability of the Supreme Court to declare Acts of Congress, and acts or actions of the presidency, unconstitutional and therefore null and void.

Appellate court A court of appeals, dealing with cases sent up to it from lower courts where one of the parties involved in the case is appealing against the lower court decision.

Original jurisdiction The power of the Supreme Court to hear a case first, before any other court. This is rare, as usually the Supreme Court only hears cases which have been referred up to it from lower courts as appeals.

Knowledge check 28

Why does a Supreme Court ruling require a constitutional amendment to overturn?

Constitutional

■ Life tenure in times of 'good behaviour'. Only one Supreme Court justice has ever been subject to impeachment hearings — Samuel Chase, 1805. However, he was acquitted of all charges. There is no retirement age.

■ A salary which 'shall not be diminished' during their time in office — a justice earns $213,900, with the chief justice earning around $10,000 extra (2009 figures).

■ Justices are appointed, not elected. They are nominated by the president and ratified by the Senate, which also goes some way to prevent a single party or branch filling the Court with their allies.

■ Separation of powers means the Supreme Court has its own power outlined within the Constitution, which ensures its sovereignty. Even if a president disagrees with a ruling, there is little in the way of pressure he can apply.

Other

■ The appointment process is rigorous and includes input from judicial experts such as the American Bar Association (ABA).

■ The Court's power of 'judicial review' is widely accepted and it is rare that a ruling is ignored by federal or state government.

The judicial review process

Judicial review is more widely accepted, understood and powerful than it is in the UK. As the Supreme Court is reviewing the constitutionality of an issue, its decisions are effectively sovereign as it is interpreting the sovereign document. Indeed the only way to overturn a Supreme Court ruling is by constitutional amendment — because the only job of the Court is to interpret the Constitution, by changing the Constitution, the interpretation must change. This power is implied, but not explicitly stated, in Article III, Section 1 of the Constitution. The Court therefore uses two key cases from which it formally 'takes' this power:

■ *Marbury* v *Madison* (1803) — a case regarding whether the new president had to honour the nomination of a judge by the previous president as it had not yet been ratified. In finding that the president did not have to honour this, the Court established its power of judicial review at federal level.

■ *Fletcher* v *Peck* (1810) — a case regarding land sales in which the Supreme Court struck down a state law for the first time, establishing its power of judicial review at state level.

> **Exam tip**
>
> Understanding *why* Supreme Court rulings are final is crucial; it was not given the power, it is that it interprets the sovereign document that is key.

Today, the Supreme Court gets sent around 8,000 cases for review each year, of which it will hear between 80 and 100. As the Supreme Court is the final court of appeal, its decision is final and there is no further appeal that can be made. The only job of the Supreme Court is to decide on the constitutionality of something — its rulings must be based in its interpretation of the Constitution alone.

If the Supreme Court finds a law or action unconstitutional, that law becomes 'null and void' — this means it does not have to be repealed, it simply ceases to be a law and cannot be enforced.

The appointment process for the Supreme Court

The appointment process for the Supreme Court (see Table 20) is not wholly outlined in the Constitution — neither is the number of justices, which is determined by Congress, although is commonly accepted as being settled at nine today.

Table 20 The appointment process to the US Supreme Court

Stage	Explanation	Examples
Vacancy	Occurs through death, retirement or impeachment of another justice	Death — Antonin Scalia, 2016 Retirement — Souter in 2009 and Stevens in 2010 Impeachment — Samuel Chase (acquitted), 1805
Search and nomination	Looking for a justice who is well qualified and suits a president's wishes	Sandra Day O'Connor came from state courts and was appointed in part because she was a woman; Sotomayor because she was a minority Presidents may look to state courts (Day O'Connor), federal courts (8/9 current justices were Circuit Court justices) or government (Kagan was the Attorney General)
ABA rating	The ABA will review and rate a candidate 'not qualified', 'qualified' or 'well qualified'	The ABA is made up of judicial experts but has no constitutional standing It is expected that justices are 'well qualified' but Thomas only achieved 'qualified' and was still nominated, although it was a close nomination and this was one of the reasons
Senate Judiciary Committee hearings and vote	A committee of 20 senators who spend days interviewing candidates as to their suitability, after which a recommendatory vote is taken	Sotomayor underwent 4 days of Senate hearings, passing 13–6; Kagan spent 3 days and also passed 13–6. It was these hearings which the Senate refused to schedule for Obama's nominee Merrick Garland This has no constitutional standing
Full Senate vote	As the Constitution requires the 'advice and consent' of Senate, the full Senate votes on a nominee	Kagan was sworn in 63–37 with only one Democrat voting against her and five Republicans voting for her

Strengths and weaknesses of the process

Weaknesses

- The process has become party political. Before 2005 it was common for justices to receive near unanimous approval if they were considered qualified (with the exception of Clarence Thomas, for other reasons), with those voting against numbering in single figures. Since 2005, the appointments of Roberts, Alito, Sotomayor and Kagan have all been notable for the party-line voting that occurred both in committee and on the floor of the Senate. The refusal to even schedule hearings for Merrick Garland had little to do with his judicial ability, but rather party politics, followed by another party line vote.

■ The president has politicised the nomination — he looks for a candidate who is likely to suit his own ideology of liberal or conservative. While he cannot guarantee the way a justice will vote, this undermines the principle of independence of the Court. Sotomayor and Kagan were both picked for being liberal, women and, in Sotomayor's case, from a minority group, as well as being legally qualified.

■ The Senate Judiciary Committee hearings have become a show. Rather than using this stage to investigate the suitability of a candidate, this televised process is used as a way for senators to grandstand. In Sotomayor's hearing, the word count was fascinating: day 1 — Sotomayor spoke 942 words out of a total of 24,117 words spoken; day 2 — 19,786 out of 47,693; day 3 — 19,100 out of 39,422; day 4 — 9,303 out of 28,698. In total, Sotomayor spoke for just 34% of the word count, which seems rather small given that it was her that the committee was investigating.

■ The role of the media undermines the process. While the process is supposed to be about appointing well-qualified candidates, the media focus on scandal, such as with Thomas and claims of sexual harassment, or Sotomayor's quote about a 'wise Latina woman', detract from this, making the process about the character not the qualifications.

■ Expectations of replacing vacancies with like for like candidates undermine the ability to pick the best candidate for the job.

Strengths

■ The lengthy and rigorous process ensures that candidates are legally qualified and capable of holding this position.

■ The role of elected officials in the process lends legitimacy to a branch which is otherwise unelected and therefore unaccountable and yet wields considerable power.

Factors influencing the president's choice of nominee

Vacancies come around so rarely, when a president does have the opportunity to fill one he must consider a range of factors for his candidate:

■ **Ideology.** While judges do not categorise themselves as 'liberal' or 'conservative', it is possible to surmise whether a justice has 'liberal' or 'conservative' leanings by looking at their past rulings. A president will want a justice who has a similar ideology to himself.

■ **Personal characteristics.** A president may wish to balance the Court in terms of gender or ethnicity; Obama appointed Sonia Sotomayor, the first Hispanic to the Court.

■ **Experience.** The appointment process is rigorous and it is embarrassing if a presidential appointee fails, so candidates are expected to have the relevant experience. Most will come from Circuit Courts but Elena Kagan came from the Justice Department.

Liberal justice A justice who interprets the Constitution more broadly in order to give the people more freedom and bring about social change.

Conservative justice A justice with a strong belief in *stare decisis*, with a narrower view of the Constitution, more likely to believe in a literal interpretation of the wording and believing in a generally smaller government.

■ **The outgoing justice.** Within reason, it is expected that a president should appoint a justice with a similar ideology to that of the outgoing justice. It hasn't always happened (Alito for Day O'Connor in 2006, for example) but is a consideration.

The current composition and ideological balance of the Supreme Court

A court is always named after its chief justice. The current court (see Table 21) is therefore the Roberts Court. After the unexpected death of Antonin Scalia in February 2016, the Supreme Court had only eight justices; his replacement was only confirmed in April 2017, 14 months later!

Table 21 The current Supreme Court

Name	Ideology	Appointed by	Age (in 2017)
John G. Roberts (chief justice)	Conservative	G. W. Bush, 2005	62
Anthony Kennedy	Swing	Reagan, 1988	80
Clarence Thomas	Conservative	H. W. Bush, 1991	68
Ruth Bader Ginsburg	Liberal	Clinton, 1993	84
Stephen Breyer	Liberal	Clinton, 1994	78
Samuel Alito	Conservative	G. W. Bush, 2006	67
Sonia Sotomayor	Liberal	Obama, 2009	62
Elena Kagan	Liberal	Obama, 2010	56
Neil Gorsuch	Conservative*	Trump, 2017	49

* Likely ideology. His impact has yet to be seen and it is not uncommon for justices to disappoint the president who appointed them by not living up to the expected ideology.

The current court retains the balance it has had for a number of decades — that is, roughly, four 'liberals', four 'conservatives' and one '**swing justice**'. While this looks like a well-balanced court, it is worth remembering that in around two-thirds of Supreme Court cases, the rulings are *not* 5–4, suggesting factors other than ideology were considered.

Even in 5–4 cases, it is not always the 'swing' justice who decides the case. Perhaps most famously, John Roberts sided with the 'liberals' in finding for Obamacare in the 2010 case of *NFIB* v *Sebelius*. In such cases, other factors may be important. The sole job of the Supreme Court is to judge a case based on the Constitution. However, as the Constitution is vague, there are two schools of thought on its application — **strict constructionist** and **loose constructionist**. In the case of *NFIB* v *Sebelius*, while it was unusual perhaps for a conservative to side with Obamacare, his reasoning was that it was not, according to the Constitution, a tax, and therefore was constitutional.

Exam tip

The cases that you study in class will be the most controversial and interesting ones; these tend to lead to 5–4 splits. Remember to show that you realise that a majority of cases are *not* decided 5–4.

Knowledge check 30

What ideology was Scalia and why was Garland a controversial replacement?

Knowledge check 31

Why are the ages of the current court of interest to Trump?

Swing justice An informal name for the justice on the Supreme Court who falls ideologically in the centre of the nine current justices.

Exam tip

Remember that 'liberal' and 'conservative' are not phrases used by justices — they are inventions of political philosophers based on how the justices have ruled. They do not guarantee the behaviour of a justice, however.

Strict/loose constructionist 'Loose construction' is a legal philosophy that favours a broad interpretation of a document's language. This term is often used to contrast with 'strict construction', a philosophy that favours looking solely at the written text of the law.

The Supreme Court and public policy

The impact of the Supreme Court on public policy in the USA

Any ruling that the Supreme Court makes has the effect of being sovereign — this is because the Court is ruling in accordance with the Constitution, the sovereign document governing US politics. Therefore, the rulings it makes, based on this document, can fundamentally change the landscape of the USA — politics, rights, laws, everything.

Table 22 The impact of the Supreme Court on areas of public policy

Area	Case	Impact
Free speech	*Snyder* v *Phelps* (2011)	Affirmed the extent of 'free speech' as protected by the 1st Amendment
Healthcare	*King* v *Burwell* (2015)	Upheld Obamacare again, allowing for its continuance
Election finance	*Citizens United* v *FEC* (2010)	Struck down some campaign finance limits as not compatible with the 1st Amendment
Abortion	*Whole Woman's Health* v *Hellerstedt* (2016)	Prevented Texas placing limits on abortion services for women
Gun control	*McDonald* v *Chicago* (2010)	Allowed for the possession of handguns, overruling a citywide ban
Affirmative action	*Fisher* v *University of Texas* (2013 and 2016)	Allowed for the use of a racially conscious admissions programme to the university

Table 22 is just a selection of cases, and is not definitive. However, in each case, what is clear is that the Supreme Court has had a fundamental impact on **public policy** in the USA — this may be upholding or striking down either state or federal law. It is also important to note that when they have decided against the government, state or federal, these rulings have been implemented despite the Supreme Court having no method to force their implementation. Texas, for example, could have ignored the 2016 ruling regarding abortion, but to do so would be to go against the Constitution as ruled by the Supreme Court, so despite disagreeing it adhered to the ruling.

Political significance debate: the role of judicial activism and judicial restraint

Judicial activism and **restraint** are ways in which we can describe the action of the Supreme Court. An activist justice will be more willing to hear cases and ensure that the outcome is based on the good of society as he or she sees it, whereas a restrained justice will believe irrespective of this, a judgement should be made on the Constitution or by looking to the elected, accountable branches of government. Both approaches are assessed in Table 23.

It is possible for a justice of either ideology to be 'active' or 'restrained' — the Roberts Court, for example, could be characterised as 'conservative activist', with rulings such as *Citizens United* overturning previous court rulings and establishing a conservative precedent.

Public policy Legislation and judicial decisions made on any policy that affect the whole of the US population.

Exam tip

Consider the word 'impact' when looking at this topic — in cases such as *King* v *Burwell*, the Supreme Court *impact* was arguably minimal, as it merely upheld a law already in action.

Judicial activism An approach to judicial decision making that holds that a justice should use his or her position to promote a desirable social end.

Judicial restraint An approach to judicial decision making that holds that a justice should defer to the executive and legislative branches, which are politically accountable to the people, and should put great stress on the principle established in previous court decisions.

Table 23 Criticisms of judicial activism and judicial restraint

Criticisms of judicial activism	Criticisms of judicial restraint
The Supreme Court is unelected and therefore unaccountable	Deference by the Supreme Court can lead to breaches of the Constitution going unchecked
It goes against the theory of separation of powers	Congress and the president often avoid the most controversial topics
It can overrule the important principle of *stare decisis*	Without interpretation, the Constitution could become outdated and irrelevant
There are limited checks on the Supreme Court to balance this power	The role of the Supreme Court is outlined in the Constitution and therefore it needs to act to uphold this
It undermines the Court's neutrality and independence	Rights apply to all, not just the majority, yet the elected branches will focus on the latter

The protection of civil liberties and rights in the USA today

Constitutional rights in the USA are protected by the Constitution, by the Bill of Rights, by subsequent constitutional amendments (see Table 24) and by rulings of the Supreme Court.

Table 24 Key constitutional rights and their protection

Amendment	Right	Supreme Court cases
1st Amendment	Free speech	*Texas* v *Johnson* (1989) guaranteed the right to flag burning based on this amendment
		Citizens United v *FEC* (2010) used this amendment to allow for greater election spending
2nd Amendment	Right to bear arms	*Chicago* v *MacDonald* (2010) and *DC* v *Heller* (2008)
5th–7th Amendments	Guarantee of trial, by jury, and right to no self-incrimination	*Miranda* v *Arizona* (1966) ruled suspects must be read their rights
8th Amendment	No cruel and unusual punishments	*Kennedy* v *Louisiana* (2008) used this to prevent the use of the death penalty as punishment for the rape of a child
13th–15th Amendments	Civil War amendments abolishing slavery, affirming due process and prohibiting the denial of the right to vote based on race	The due process clause has been used to allow for, and defend, abortion (*Roe* v *Wade*, 1973 and *Whole Woman's Health* v *Hellerstedt*, 2016) and gay marriage (*Obergefell* v *Hodges*, 2015)
19th and 26th Amendments	Right to vote for women and those aged over 18	

The effectiveness of the protection of rights by the Supreme Court is always debatable. For example, while *Snyder* v *Phelps* upheld the right to free speech of the Westboro Baptist Church, it arguably diminished the right to privacy of the Phelps family. Equally, that the Supreme Court has ruled does not always mean that states or even the federal government will always adhere to this ruling. In the *Hamdi* v *Rumsfeld* ruling of 2005, the federal government only conceded limited changes to Guantanamo Bay following its loss in this case.

Stare decisis This doctrine is built on the idea of standing by decided cases, upholding precedents and maintaining former adjudications. Thus it tends to favour the status quo. This is the opposite of the 'Living Constitution' approach.

Exam tip

For each criticism, the AO2 analysis is crucial — *why* is it a criticism and just how bad is it? This kind of well-argued judgement is what ensures top marks.

Constitutional rights The rights specifically outlined for citizens within the US Constitution, Bill of Rights and subsequent amendments.

Knowledge check 32

What are the five freedoms guaranteed in Article I?

Race and rights in contemporary US politics

The US Declaration of Independence proudly stated that 'all men are created equal'. Despite this apparently 'self-evident' truth, for decades of American history, rights were based on the colour of their skin.

Racial rights campaigns

The passage of the Civil War amendments from 1865 to 1870 supposedly guaranteed the rights of the newly freed slaves. In practice, Jim Crow laws ensured that for continuing decades they remained disenfranchised and discriminated against. Even the Supreme Court allowed for segregation in 1896 provided such segregation was 'equal' — in practice, this was rarely the case.

The civil rights movement through the 1950s and 1960s, spearheaded by people like Martin Luther King Jnr and Malcolm X, took radically differing approaches to winning equality. Ultimately, the passage of the 1964 Civil Rights Act outlawing discrimination based on race, colour, religion or sex, as well as the 1954 Supreme Court ruling of *Brown* v *Topeka* reversing the 'separate but equal' ruling, should have ensured equality.

Methods and influence

Groups fighting for equality in racial rights have a wide range of methods:

- Filing amicus curiae briefs with the Supreme Court or even taking cases to court, such as BAMN in 2014 challenging a ban on affirmative action in the Michigan state constitution
- Protesting — protests range from standing on the steps of the Supreme Court or more violent demonstrations such as some of those which occurred following the shootings in Ferguson
- Holding conferences — the National Council of La Raza's annual conference carries enough weight to try and gain action, such as labelling Obama the 'deporter-in-chief'
- Using social media, which has shown notable growth, for example the #blacklivesmatter campaign

Effectiveness of campaigns

- Supreme Court successes in some cases such as *Fisher* v *Texas*, but not in *Schuette* v *BAMN*
- Failure to achieve congressional action on immigration
- Obama did pass DAPA and DACA expansions, but while the original programme remains, the expansions were struck down by the Supreme Court
- High-profile occurrences such as the shootings of Treyvon Martin and Michael Brown have arguably furthered division and highlighted remaining inequalities
- Only 52 members or 9.6% of the 115th Congress are African American and 8.3% (45 members) are Hispanic — a record high but still not accurately reflecting the makeup of the US population
- Sonia Sotomayor is the first Hispanic woman on the Supreme Court

Exam tip

It is important not to read 'race' as 'African American'. You should certainly know about Hispanic voters, and potentially other groups too.

Knowledge check 33

What is the translation of 'amicus curiae'?

Voting rights, affirmative action and representation

Voting rights, while constitutionally established, remain controversial. Rulings such as *Shelby County* v *Holder* (2013) reduced the power of the federal government to challenge electoral practices it deemed to be discriminatory. This is notable given that, just a few years earlier, Arizona passed SB1070 requiring Hispanics to register and carry identification. While cases such as *Grutter* v *Bollinger* (2003) and *Texas* v *Fisher* (2013) allow for some, limited, continued use of affirmative action, it is increasingly being challenged.

Interpretations and debates of the US Supreme Court and civil rights

The political v judicial nature of the Supreme Court

While the neutrality of the Supreme Court is guaranteed by the US Constitution, in practice, it can be difficult to see whether the Court is a judicial or political actor. Table 25 looks at the arguments.

Table 25 Key arguments on the political v judicial nature of the Supreme Court

Arguments that the Court is judicial in nature	Arguments that the Court is political in nature
All rulings are made with reference to the US Constitution, not personal opinion	Rulings have a political impact, affecting the laws from elected branches
Justices are expected to have legal and/or judicial experience	Justices are appointed through an entirely political process
The Court has no enforcement power, and so relies on being seen as judicial for its rulings to be accepted	Justices can be identified as 'liberal' and 'conservative', suggesting an ideological leaning
Only around a third of cases are decided 5–4, suggesting a good deal of legal agreement	The Court accepts amicus curiae briefings from politically interested groups
There are plenty of examples where a justice has not ruled as expected from their labelled ideology	It can seem that the Court will choose to hear cases or not based on the political climate and public opinion
The Court applies legal principles such as *stare decisis*	Some cases are about politics directly, e.g. *Bush* v *Gore* (2000)

Living Constitution ideology as against originalism

The use of the Constitution as a basis to make Supreme Court decisions is itself controversial. The document is over 200 years old and the Founding Fathers could not have envisioned the world in which we live today. Therefore, it could be argued that for the document to remain relevant, as a 'Living Constitution', it needs to be interpreted — free speech in the age of the internet is a good example. However, the act of interpreting this document means that the USA will evolve away from some of the ideals laid down by the Founding Fathers, upheld by those supporting originalism. Many of the arguments surrounding these debates are similar to those regarding judicial activism and restraint. In addition, however, it can be debated as to which is more applicable to the US Constitution today (see Table 26).

Affirmative action A policy of favouring historically disadvantaged members of a community.

Living Constitution The idea that the Constitution is an evolutionary document that can change over time through reinterpretation by the Supreme Court (linked to loose constructionism).

Originalism The idea that the meaning of the US Constitution is fixed and should not be subject to interpretation.

Exam tip

Do not make the basic mistake of assuming conservative justices will be restrained, strict constructionist and originalist, and liberals the opposite. Each of these terms must be understood separately.

Table 26 Arguments surrounding Living Constitutionalism and originalism

The Constitution is, or should be, 'living'	The Constitution is still, or should be, 'original'
Without interpretation, the document will become irrelevant in the modern world	The Constitution includes an amendment process to allow for its evolution as needed
If the Supreme Court does not interpret the document, politically biased elected branches will; this could disadvantage minorities	If the Constitution can be changed by nine unelected justices, there is no accountability either to the people or elected branches
The Constitution provides underlying principles for the USA; for these to be upheld in a changing world, it needs to be interpreted	The Supreme Court's power comes from a court case of its own, not the Constitution, therefore it does not have the right to change the Constitution
If the Founding Fathers wanted to prevent the interpretation of the document, they would have been more specific	A flexible constitution can be deliberately misinterpreted or used for political ends, rather than provide the protections intended by the Founding Fathers

Effectiveness of rights protection

Some civil and constitutional rights have been routinely upheld by the Supreme Court even in the face of public anger — flag burning (*Texas* v *Johnson*, 1989) and *Citizens United* v *FEC*, 2010) are good examples. The latter was condemned by President Obama as 'opening the floodgates' to effectively allow corporations to 'buy' elections; nonetheless the Supreme Court upheld it, and even furthered it in *McCutcheon* v *FEC* (2014). It is worthy of consideration, however, that the 2010 case overturned the precedent set in 2003 — *McConnell* v *FEC*, in which the Supreme Court ruled the exact opposite. Yet this itself was an overruling of the 1976 *Buckley* v *Valeo* case! It seems, therefore, that the Supreme Court's 'effectiveness' at upholding rights depends on which side you fall.

Table 27 looks at some other examples of rights cases. In assessing the effectiveness of the Court's role, it is also worth considering how much power it actually has.

Knowledge check 34

What is the principle of *stare decisis*?

Table 27 Selected examples of controversial rights

Rights of minorities	*Fisher* v *University of Texas* (2016) *Grutter* v *Bollinger* (2003)	In both cases, the use of affirmative action to support minority rights could be argued to come at a disadvantage to the white American plaintiff
Rights of detainees	*Hamdi* v *Rumsfeld* (2004) *Hamden* v *Rumsfeld* (2006) *Boumediene* v *Bush* (2008)	Each of these cases concerned access to courts by those held in Guantanamo Bay In each case the Court ruled to uphold detainees' rights but the facts that there were three consecutive cases and that Guantanamo is still open suggest the Court has not been entirely effective in their defence
Cruel and unusual punishment	*Kennedy* v *Louisiana* (2008) *Baze* v *Rees* (2008)	On the one hand, a series of cases in the twenty-first century placed limits on those who could be executed. The Kennedy case prevented a child rapist being put to death On the other hand, the Court upheld the use of lethal injection (Baze), and subsequent controversies have ensued over the 'cruel' nature of this method in cases such as that of Clayton Lockett (2014)

Exam tip

It is crucial here to understand what 'effectiveness' means, and for whom. In each case, both sides claim they have the Constitution on their side; one is bound to be disappointed.

The extent of the Court's powers and the effectiveness of checks and balances

The key power of the Supreme Court, judicial review, comes from the cases of *Marbury* v *Madison* and *Fletcher* v *Peck* rather than from the Constitution. For this, and a range of other reasons, the actual power that the Court holds could be questioned:

■ It has no power of initiation — it cannot bring cases to itself but must wait for them to be referred from other courts.

■ It has no power of enforcement — beyond the nine justices, it has no police or armed forces to carry out its rulings; it relies entirely on the elected branches for this.

■ It can have its rulings overturned through a constitutional amendment; this has, however, only happened once (the 16th Amendment).

■ It does seem to be responsive to the public and elected branches in some areas — the lack of gun control cases for a good number of years could be argued to be because it was by its nature very controversial. Equally, amicus curiae briefs from the public or even Congress are accepted — in *McDonald* v *Chicago* (2010) Congress filed its largest ever amicus curiae brief with 251 members of the House of Representatives and 58 senators having signed it to support McDonald.

Despite this, there is some claim that the Supreme Court is an '**imperial judiciary**':

■ The Supreme Court's word is invariably final — there has only ever been one constitutional amendment used to overturn one of its rulings; in addition, the amendment process is hugely difficult.

■ While it cannot bring cases, it does choose from 8,000 each year, giving it huge power over those it hears and those it chooses not to, especially as it is likely to pick the cases of greatest significance.

■ It has and can overrule the elected branches of government, including the states. *Obergefell* v *Hodges* (2015), for example, legalised gay marriage even in states where a majority of the electorate were against it.

■ It has even effectively decided the president — in *Bush* v *Gore* (2000), by denying the recount, the Court effectively gave the election to Bush.

■ The Supreme Court acts without accountability as justices are appointed for life and no one justice has ever been successfully impeached.

■ It has effectively created new rights not outlined in the Constitution, such as abortion and gay marriage.

Imperial judiciary
A judiciary that is all-powerful and on which checks and balances are weak and ineffective.

Knowledge check 35

What is the upper age limit for US Supreme Court justices?

Assessing affirmative action and immigration reform

Despite advances, the USA remains a deeply divided nation, as evidenced above. Table 28 lists some successes and failures of efforts to increase equality.

Table 28 Successes and failures of equality in the USA

Successes	Failures
Obama's original DACA of 2012 still remains	DAPA and expanded DACA was struck down in *US* v *Texas* (2016)
Affirmative action has been upheld in limited forms through Supreme Court cases	The Gang-of-Eight failed to get the comprehensive immigration reform bill through the House of Representatives

→

Successes	Failures
The representation of minorities in Congress continues to improve	High-profile shootings have raised the failures of racial equality into the national spotlight
Arizona's SB1070 was largely struck down by the Supreme Court	The election of Trump, with rhetoric such as 'build a wall', suggests divisions remain

Comparisons with the UK

Basis for and relative extent of the Courts' powers

The US Supreme Court has a more substantial basis for its power than its UK counterpart — while the power of judicial review is not enshrined in the Constitution, the body itself is and its power is accepted. The UK Supreme Court, in comparison, gains power from the 2005 Constitutional Reform Act. Whereas the US Constitution essentially makes the US Supreme Court quasi-sovereign, interpreting the sovereign document, the UK court relies on parliamentary sovereignty for its existence, which could be (albeit unlikely) revoked.

This, therefore, has an impact on the power of the two courts. While the US Supreme Court can only be overturned by altering the sovereign document, the UK Supreme Court has no legal sovereignty and the Court could be ignored by government. In reality, however, the courts are perhaps more similar in power than they appear — quickly contrasting cases such as those on Brexit and DAPA, we see two executive-sponsored initiatives struck down by their respective court and yet both courts were adhered to.

Relative independence of the Supreme Court in the USA and the UK

The US Supreme Court is protected by the Constitution — its power and existence are guaranteed irrespective of the government. Comparatively, the UK court depends on parliamentary statute for its existence, which could perhaps undermine its independence. However, there are similarities in their guarantee of independence:

- In both countries, justices are appointed for life, although in the UK there is an upper age limit.
- The appointment process in both countries tries to ensure some independence. In the USA, the president and Congress must work together but the role of the ABA ensures some legal expertise; in the UK, the Judicial Appointments Commission is politically independent.
- The pay for judges is equally protected. In the UK it is suggested by an independent body, which the government usually accepts, and in the USA there is protection for pay built into the Constitution.
- In both countries, justices are expected to have legal backgrounds and training, thus ensuring they are not merely parachuted in by the government.

Nonetheless, the lack of constitutional protections in the UK has raised questions, with Lord Phillips claiming in 2011 that the court had no guaranteed budget but relied on 'persuading' the Ministry of Justice to give it money, which could undermine its independence.

Racial equality Equal regard to all races. It can refer to a belief in biological equality of all human races and to social equality for people of different races. In the USA, there remain calls for desegregation and voter registration in the south, and better jobs, housing and school integration in the north.

Exam tip

Understanding sovereignty is key to understanding the power of each court — they may act similarly but the US Supreme Court has more legal power.

Effectiveness of the protection of rights in each country

The effectiveness of the US Supreme Court (outlined above) is clearly rooted in the Constitution — for rights not guaranteed within this document, their protection cannot be guaranteed. In the UK, while protections are perhaps not so concrete, the Human Rights Act (1998), rooted in the European Convention on Human Rights (ECHR) and enforceable in the European Court of Justice, there is a greater range of rights which are protected. While this may only be a statute law, and is therefore revocable, the likelihood of it being revoked seems remote, especially without replacement.

In both countries, one of the flaws of rights protection could arguably be the longevity of the legal process, and the cost. Nonetheless, in the UK, if the Supreme Court does not adequately protect a right, there are other avenues that can be pursued — the European Union, the ECHR or even Parliament. The quasi-sovereign nature of the US Supreme Court means a ruling from it effectively spells the end to a case of rights protection — if you are ruled against, that's it.

However, it is far easier to challenge the government in the USA as Supreme Court rulings hold more weight. In the UK, while sovereignty rests with Parliament, the government can choose to ignore the Supreme Court with greater ease, although probably with just as much public outcry.

Effectiveness of interest groups in the protection of rights in the USA and UK

The access points for interest groups, while growing in the UK, are more numerous and established in the USA. While groups in the UK have funded cases, such as the Christian groups involved in the Asher's Bakery case, in the USA it is possible for a group to be far more intimately embedded within the judicial process through amicus curiae briefs and the bringing of court cases. In the UK, this has meant a group may be effective, but through other means (e.g. e-petitions) rather than through the judicial process.

Rational, cultural and structural approaches

Due to the precarious nature of the courts in both countries, being reliant to some extent on the executive and legislative branches for enforcement, the courts could perhaps be argued to act rationally, or selfishly. For example, the unexpected vote of John Roberts to support Obamacare in *NFIB* v *Sebelius* could be argued to have been to ensure the security of the Court in the face of a president who won an election on this pledge. Equally, in the UK, the 2017 Brexit ruling could arguably have been for the opposite, but still selfish, reason — to assert judicial independence from the government.

There is a clear cultural impact inherent within the rulings, however. While the UK justices are perhaps less easily divided ideologically, the fact that the Brexit ruling was 8–3 suggests more was at play than simply a black-and-white case of law. The division of US justices into 'liberal/conservative', 'activist/restrained' or 'loose/strict constructionists' suggests that cultural factors are considered.

Structural theory, however, is perhaps the most important to understanding a branch of government which, in both countries, is arguably less significant than other branches

Exam tip

When arguing 'rationally' for the Supreme Court, it could be arguing that justices vote selfishly in accordance to their personal preference, or to protect the Court and therefore their job or role.

of government. Their power comes from their independence and the way in which this is viewed both within a system of checks and balances and by the public as guardians of their rights. This both enhances and limits their power, both being relatively well regarded yet reliant on the power of the elected branches to carry out their rulings. This could help to explain their rulings on occasion; even the Brexit ruling could be viewed through this lens, allowing the government to uphold its legitimacy by making the ruling through Parliament while upholding judicial power too.

Summary

- The power of the US Supreme Court is rooted both in the Constitution and in *Marbury* v *Madison* (1803) and *Fletcher* v *Peck* (1810).
- The independence of the Supreme Court is guaranteed through life tenure, guaranteed pay and quasi-sovereignty taken from the Constitution.
- While the Supreme Court is governed by checks and balances, its rulings are usually upheld despite its lack of enforcement power, granting it considerable power.
- Protection of rights varies across circumstances and cases, but has certainly come under closer scrutiny since the growing threat of terrorism and the advent of Guantanamo Bay.
- Race rights have been considerably advanced but continue to raise important questions within the branches of government, especially given recent impasses regarding immigration reform and high-profile shooting victims.

■ US democracy and participation

Electoral systems in the USA

Presidential elections and their significance

Presidential nominations: the primary and caucus process

Presidential elections have two stages:

1. The presidential nomination process (also known as primaries and caucuses, or primaries for short). A primary election involves candidates from the same party competing with each other in a public vote to decide which candidate will stand in the election for office.

2. The presidential election process (also known as the Electoral College).

Key features of the primary process

- Candidates compete within states, not in a single national vote.
- Different states vote on different dates, starting with Iowa.
- Each state has a number of delegates, with candidates competing to win these delegates in each state. The more votes a candidate gets, the more delegates they capture.

- The delegates attend a party meeting (national party convention) and cast votes to determine who will be the presidential candidate for that party.
- A candidate requires over 50% of the votes to become the presidential nominee.

In 2016 the Democratic primary was a two-horse race between Hillary Clinton and Bernie Sanders. The Republican contest contained the widest field ever, giving voters a huge choice of policy, ideology and character. Jeb Bush, a moderate Republican, was one of the favourites to win, with other notable candidates Ted Cruz and Marco Rubio representing social conservatism and Donald Trump entering the race as a political outsider.

Other features of primaries and caucuses

- **Voter eligibility.** Different states have different rules about voting, with states holding open, closed, semi-open or caucus elections.
- **Translating votes to delegates.** In 2016, while the Democrats had a proportional rule (delegates are awarded in each state in proportion to the votes they receive), the Republicans had a proportional rule in some states and used winner-takes-all in others.
- **Unpledged delegates.** Some delegates are able to attend a party convention because they are important party officials, such as former members of Congress. In the GOP primaries in 2016, these delegates still had to vote according to voting patterns in the state they are from. In the Democrat Party, however, these delegates are unpledged, accounting for 15% of the total. They can use their own judgement as to how they vote.
- **One-party primary.** In 2012, only the Republicans held primaries, with no Democrat challenger to President Obama.

Criticisms

- **Specific procedures.** States using caucus elections create low turnout because they do not use private voting but a public debate and vote, which many people will not commit to. Open primaries allow for negative voting or spoiling tactics, where a supporter of one party can vote in the other party's primary. Closed primaries prevent this, with supporters of a party voting only in their own party primary.
- **Timing.** Voting takes place over several months, with early states having greater influence and later states often being disenfranchised because the decision is made before all states have voted.
- **Party divides.** The process causes divisions within each party and can make it harder for them to win the presidential election.

Benefits

- **Voter choice.** The process allows voters to choose which one of several candidates will be the candidate for their preferred party. Voters can select on the basis of ideology, experience, personal ability or social characteristics.
- **Voter education.** Primaries create a longer campaign period. Internal party debates focus on key issues of concern and alternative strategies to deal with them.
- **Proven party candidates.** Primaries benefit parties because they allow a popular candidate to become the nominee for their party. This increases the chances of the party winning the presidential election.

Knowledge check 36

What is the difference between the presidential nomination process and the presidential election?

Knowledge check 37

What is the difference between a primary and a caucus vote?

Invisible primaries

Invisible primaries are an important part of the voting process even though no voting takes place. Candidates try to put themselves in the strongest position to compete successfully when voting begins in the primaries. This is achieved by raising funds, developing name recognition and hopefully a loyal following, as well as an effective campaign infrastructure. Invisible primaries increase in intensity over time as more time and money is spent on campaigning.

Funding levels and opinion polls affect voter perceptions. Those who perform badly in invisible primaries can lose credibility, with voters less likely to vote for them. The invisible primaries can force less successful candidates to drop out.

For the 2016 GOP elections, Senator Ted Cruz was the first to declare in March 2015, some 10 months before the first vote in the Iowa caucus. Donald Trump entered the race after most candidates had already declared in June 2015 and despite being initially dismissed as an outsider, gained media attention, quickly becoming a favourite to win.

Invisible primary
The period before primary voting in which candidates attempt to establish themselves as potential winners by raising funding and trying to secure public support.

National party conventions

Each party holds a national party convention at the end of the primary process. In theory, conventions select the presidential candidate for that party but this role has become redundant since national primaries were created in 1968. All delegates from the primary process attend. The nominee (the person chosen to run for the presidency) is known before the convention, with one candidate typically receiving well over 50% of the delegates before all states have voted.

The traditional or superficial roles of conventions are to:
- select the presidential candidate
- select the running mate
- determine the party platform for the presidential election

Their modern or significant role is to:
- launch the presidential election campaign
- enthuse party activists
- reunite the party

In 2016 both parties chose swing states in order to boost their support in these areas.

The GOP Convention in Ohio and the Democratic Convention in Philadelphia

- Ted Cruz used his speech to urge voters to 'vote your conscience' rather than vote for Trump.
- Trump's final night speech attracted more viewers than Clinton's speech at the Philadelphia Convention where she has appeared united on stage with her main rival Sanders.
- Trump's policy promises conflicted with some of those developed by the Republican National Committee.
- The vice-presidential candidates of Mike Pence and Tim Kaine were announced by Trump and Clinton ahead of the conventions.

The Electoral College

The Electoral College is the name given to the process of electing the president. The process has the following key features:

- Voting takes place within states all on the same day.
- Each state is given a value. (The Constitution says that the value in each state shall be the same as the number of congressmen and senators from that state.)
- This value represents a number of delegates who make up the Electoral College: a group of people who will later vote to decide who the president will be.
- Each state uses a winner-takes-all system in which the candidate with the most votes gets all the delegates for that state.
- In order to become the president, the Constitution requires a candidate to receive over 50% of the Electoral College votes (ECV).

Whichever candidate has secured over 50% of delegates is expected to win and this is known as soon as the results come in. Technically, however, the candidate has not won until the Electoral College votes, some weeks later. With 21 states not legally compelling the delegates to vote according to the public vote in their state, delegates could switch their vote.

Table 29 Election results 2016

	Clinton (Democrat)	Trump (Republican)
Popular vote	65,845,063	62,980,160
Percentage popular vote	48.0	45.9
Electoral college vote	227	304
States won	20	30

Assessment of the Electoral College

The Electoral College reflects the dominant values of the Founding Fathers. While they wanted the general public to have an input in determining who holds power, they also distrusted the people. Establishing an electoral college provided three major advantages which are more difficult to justify today:

- prevention of mob rule, limiting the control of the public
- protecting the power of states, especially smaller states by over-representing them
- producing a clear winner, using the Electoral College points rather than the popular vote to determine who has won

There are several criticisms of the current system compared to a national popular vote in which people vote directly for presidential candidates in a US-wide vote:

- **The winner loses.** It is possible for one candidate to receive the most popular votes but for another candidate to become the president by winning the most ECV. This can be seen as highly undemocratic and has occurred twice recently, in 2000 when Bush (not Gore) became president and again in 2016 when Trump became president even though he received nearly 3 million fewer votes than Clinton (see Table 29).
- **Rogue delegates.** Sometimes known as 'faithless electors', the ability of delegates to ignore public opinion is a major concern for democracy. In 2016 seven delegates did not vote according to voting patterns in their state, five of whom were supposed to vote for Clinton and two who were supposed to vote for Trump.

- **Over-representation of small states.** The Constitution deliberately over-represents small states by making the value of each state equal to the number of congressmen (which is roughly proportional to population) plus two. A vote in Wyoming (the state with the lowest population) is worth more than a vote in California (with the largest).
- **The focus on swing states.** Electoral success is determined by a small number of states which swing from one party to another. In safe states, one party is guaranteed success because of the high winning margin at the last election. This means that candidates tend to focus resources and policies on swing states, including Ohio and Florida in 2016.

The party system

The USA has a strong two-**party system** with only two parties dominating presidential and congressional elections. All presidents since the Civil War have been Democrats or Republicans. There is limited evidence for a multi-party system, with the third-placed candidate Gary Johnson (Libertarian), receiving just 3.3% of the vote in 2016. A presidential system in which only one person is elected discourages people from voting for third parties which are likely to lose. In addition, primaries have strengthened the two-party system. Any non-Democrat or non-Republican candidate may choose to run in either of these party primaries as a more effective way of winning. Arguably this is exactly what Trump did by running as a political outsider in the Republican Party primaries.

Party system The nature of parties and in particular the number of parties which have significant political power such as a two-party or a multi-party system.

Incumbency and second-term presidents

The incumbent (the person in office) appears to have an advantage in presidential elections. In the 32 US presidential elections where the incumbent stood, 22 of those candidates have won (68.7%).

Incumbency advantages include the following:

- Using their role to increase public support, for example among key voter groups. Obama achieved this in his first term with the appointment of the first Hispanic justice, as well as focusing on immigration reform. His share of the Hispanic vote increased in the 2012 elections. It could also involve claiming responsibility for success, such as economic growth or military achievements.
- Making use of electoral experience. Sitting presidents have already won one election and can use the knowledge gained to compete more effectively. In addition, sitting presidents can usually raise more money than rivals. The last sitting president to raise less than their challenger was George Bush Snr, who was defeated by Bill Clinton.
- Name recognition. Presidents usually find it easier to gain attention than rivals, partly by using their role as head of state to address the nation. Presidents have higher authority than their rivals, especially when responding to major events where the public may look for leadership.

Despite this, incumbency may not always be at an advantage:

- Presidents may take the blame either for their own policies or for events in general. The weak state of the economy did not help President Bush Snr in the election against Clinton in 1992. Presidents find their record under attack.

- Incumbents do not always raise more than challengers. In addition, money does not guarantee success. While there was no incumbent candidate in 2016, the incumbent party lost the presidency, even though Clinton outspent Trump considerably.
- Challengers gain considerable publicity, especially given the use of television debates which create a level playing field with candidates appearing on the same stage. Presidents may make campaign mistakes such as Bush Snr checking his watch during the TV debates against Clinton.

Campaign finance

The role of campaign finance

During elections money is donated by individuals, interest groups and corporations, with candidates sometimes providing some of their own funding. Some money is donated to other groups who support or oppose a particular party or politician.

Campaign finance expenditure is mainly spent on advertising, as well as on campaign staff and travel. It has played an increasing role in US elections with a huge rise in expenditure in presidential elections over recent years. The role of campaign finance has led to a number of concerns:

A Excessive influence of major donors

B Inequality of expenditure (between presidential candidates)

C A lack of openness about who is donating to whom

Campaign finance legislation

In order to overcome these concerns, campaign finance legislation has been passed. This refers to any law which attempts to regulate the role of money in US elections. There are two major Acts:

Federal Election Campaign Act (FECA) 1974

1 Limits campaign contributions. A private individual could only donate $1,000 and a group could only donate $2,500.

2 Creates federal funding of presidential elections. For every dollar a candidate raises, they are given a dollar by the federal government.

3 Creates Political Action Committees (PACs) which have to be created by any group that wants to donate money to a campaign. This is legally registered with the Federal Election Commission (FEC) and all donations are made public.

4 Creates a maximum campaign expenditure for each presidential candidate.

Candidates are only subject to maximum expenditure limits if they take federal funding. In 2012 and 2016 no candidate did this. Modern candidates are therefore free to spend as much money as they can raise.

The use of soft money demonstrated the failure of FECA to be sufficiently effective. One way around the regulations was for pressure groups to develop issue adverts, which highlight an issue of concern without explicitly supporting or opposing a candidate. This was not then counted as money spent or donated even if it was intended to influence electoral outcomes. Subsequent legislation was passed in order to reduce the influence of soft money.

Exam tip

In essays, students are expected to show an awareness of competing arguments and to make judgements about the strength of those arguments. You can do this by discussing why arguments such as those above are strong or weak.

Campaign finance Any money raised, donated or spent in order to influence electoral outcomes.

Political Action Committee (PAC) Any group that wishes to donate money has to create its own PAC, a legally registered organisation which is responsible for conforming to campaign finance regulations.

Knowledge check 39

Taking each of the key FECA provisions in turn, does that provision attempt to solve A, B or C above?

Soft money/hard money Soft money refers to money spent or raised which cannot be regulated by campaign finance laws. Hard money refers to regulated money.

Bipartisan Campaign Reform Act (BCRA) 2003

The BCRA, also known as McCain–Feingold after the authors of the Act, had the following provisions:

1 Banned soft-money donations to national parties, which meant that all money raised or spent by parties is subject to the limits of FECA.

2 Issue adverts could not be funded directly by unions or corporations.

3 Issue adverts which mention a candidate's name cannot be shown within 60 days of an election. If they are shown, they have to be approved by one of the candidates and are therefore subject to FECA limits.

The impact of Citizens United

The BCRA was challenged in the Supreme Court in the case of *Citizens United* v *FEC* (2010). The Supreme Court overturned key parts of the Act on the basis of the 1st Amendment right to freedom of expression. This ruling opened the way for unlimited campaign adverts at election time and led to the creation of **SuperPACs**. These organisations can raise and spend unlimited amounts of money at election time. Instead of donating money to a candidate (which is subject to FECA limits on donations and expenditure), individuals and interest groups donate to a SuperPAC which then spends money campaigning for a candidate. As long as the SuperPAC and the candidate do not coordinate their efforts then there are no finance limits. This is significant in a number of ways:

SuperPACs
Organisations which influence electoral outcomes usually through advertising but which are not limited by campaign finance law because they are separate from candidates and parties.

■ There has been a major rise in campaign expenditure. Both the 2012 presidential election and the 2014 midterm elections were more expensive than previous elections (although the total spend for 2016 was lower than 2008 and 2012).

■ There is significant inequality of expenditure, as some candidates receive more SuperPAC support than others. This was particularly noticeable in the 2016 Republican primaries, in which the Jeb Bush SuperPAC, Right to Rise, easily outspent all other SuperPACS supporting Republican candidates.

■ Corporate influence has increased. Most money is donated by corporations, allowing the interests of wealthy donors to influence candidates eager to increase their positive publicity.

■ Adverts have become more negative or misleading. With campaigns being run independently from presidential candidates, there is less desire for respect for opposing candidates and an emphasis on all-out attack, sometimes of a personal nature.

SuperPACs undermine representative democracy because they distort the election process, giving greater advantages to well-funded candidates. In addition, they could undermine pluralist democracy and instead promote elitism. Power becomes concentrated in the hands of a small elite of established politicians and corporations rather than being shared.

Parties in the USA: key ideas and principles

Democratic and Republican policy

The USA is dominated by two parties. The Democrats are often described as the liberal party, with more left-wing or socially progressive ideas. The Republican Party is associated with conservatism or more right-wing policies.

Policy differences

Table 30 sets out key differences between the two parties in terms of social and moral policy, the national economy and federal welfare.

Table 30 Democratic and Republican Party policy differences

	Democratic Party	Republican Party
Social and moral policy	■ More liberal approach to social and moral policy ■ Stronger support for the protection of civil rights ■ Historically supported rights for women and racial minorities, including a more liberal approach to immigration ■ Typically supportive of transgender rights	■ More conservative approach to social and moral policy ■ Less supportive of civil rights laws such as the Voting Rights Act 1965 ■ More likely to oppose abortion rights ■ In 2016 the majority of Republicans in Congress opposed Obama's measures for transgender rights. Republicans have typically opposed immigration reform to give more rights to illegal immigrants
National economy	■ Tend to favour a more active role for the government in the national economy ■ Include higher taxes on the wealthy, higher public expenditure and greater federal regulations (for example on corporations) ■ Aim to promote improved life chances for those with lower socioeconomic status ■ 2016 support for an increased federal minimum wage	■ Republicans tend to favour a reduced role for the government in the national economy ■ Typically will cut income tax, especially for the wealthy, and cut federal expenditure and services ■ Emphasise individual effort and competition, with government seen as a limit to individual economic freedom ■ Republicans have pursued major expenditure cuts with Speaker Paul Ryan aiming to achieve a balanced budget
Federal welfare	■ Favour increased provision of federal welfare ■ Higher expenditure on health and education policy as well as benefits for the less well off ■ Promote the idea of social justice to overcome the unfairness of the social and economic system of the USA ■ The Affordable Care Act, providing health insurance for most of the 46 million uninsured Americans and the provision of food stamps are key Democrat policies	■ Republicans typically support some federal welfare provision but emphasise personal responsibility ■ Typically want to reduce welfare provision ■ Welfare provision is equated with big government and a restriction on individual freedom ■ No Republicans in Congress supported the Affordable Care Act. In 2017 Republicans worked on a plan to dismantle the Act

Exam tip

Students sometimes limit their marks for party questions because they only talk about party policies in a very general way. Make sure you know specific details of contemporary examples of the policies of the parties.

Party factions

Democrats

The main conflict in the Democratic Party has been between the liberal (or progressive) faction and the moderate faction. Conservative Democrats, once prominent in the party, are in major decline and have limited impact on the party. This can be seen in the 2016 presidential primary contest between progressive/liberal Bernie Sanders and moderate Hillary Clinton.

Key points about the liberal, moderate and conservative factions are outlined in Table 31.

Factions These are organised subgroups within a party, usually based around different ideological goals or emphases.

Table 31 Factions in the Democratic Party

Liberals	Moderates	Conservative Democrats
■ Tend to promote the main values of the party to a greater extent than moderates ■ More critical of capitalism and corporations, calling for a stronger government role in the economy than moderate Democrats ■ Much less willing to compromise with Republican policies than moderates ■ Recently, the liberal wing has been particularly vocal about the dangers of free trade and the need to protect American workers, for example strongly opposing the Trans Pacific Partnership (TPP) ■ Represented by figures such as Elizabeth Warren, Bernie Sanders and Nancy Pelosi, all holding important positions in the party	■ Tend to favour key Democrat goals with less intensity or to a lesser extent For example, being less critical of capitalism and corporations than liberal Democrats ■ More willing to compromise with Republican goals, such as President Clinton's adoption of the Republican goal of balanced budget politics in the 1990s ■ Favour free trade as desirable for the US economy, as seen in Obama's support for TPP ■ More likely to support defence expenditure and military intervention ■ Represented by Obama, Bill Clinton and Hillary Clinton, three of the most senior figures in the Democratic Party in recent years	■ Also referred to as Blue Dog Democrats, this faction has become considerably less important. As of January 2017 there were only 13 Blue Dogs left in the House ■ Once a dominant faction, with solid Democrat support in the south until the civil rights movement of the 1950s and 1960s ■ Particularly conservative on social and moral issues, for example favouring gun ownership and strong immigration controls ■ One of its co-chairs, Representative Jim Costa, voted in favour of a bill restricting Syrian refugee entry into the USA in 2015, supported the Keystone Pipeline and was initially reluctant to support the Affordable Care Act

Republicans

Key points about the main factions in the Republican Party factions are set out in Table 32.

Table 32 Factions in the Republican Party

Social conservatives	Fiscal conservatives	Moderates
■ This faction focuses on areas of social and moral policy, such as opposing gay and transgender rights, abortion and immigration, while supporting guns ■ It is mostly based around conservative Christian, evangelical views ■ This faction has grown considerably in recent years ■ It was behind plans to defund Planned Parenthood in 2016 and 2017 ■ Represented by figures such as Ted Cruz	■ This faction focused on the economy as its main priority, with the aim to reduce the role of the US government ■ Advocates major tax and expenditure cuts as well as deregulation ■ A dominant faction in the party acting as the main driving force for Republican economic policy, especially in opposition to Obama policies ■ Reflected in the influence of the Freedom Caucus ■ Represented by figures such as Paul Ryan	■ Will tend to support the ideals of social or fiscal conservatism to a lesser extent ■ Are more willing to compromise with Democrat policies/ideas ■ Is organised under the Main Street Partnership, with over 70 congressional members in January 2017 ■ Particularly moderate Republicans such as Senator Susan Collins are known as RINOs — Republicans in name only ■ Has been a successful faction, with presidents George Bush and Donald Trump having moderate elements. Bush's high expenditure and Trump's proposed $1 trillion infrastructure plan are in direct conflict with fiscal conservatism

Knowledge check 40

What are the three main policy areas which can be used to compare Democrat and Republican policies?

Exam tip

An individual does not necessarily neatly fit into one of these three factions. Some Republicans may be both socially and fiscally conservative, for example.

Arguably the Republican Party has been more factionalised than the Democratic Party in recent years, especially with the growth of a more hard-line conservative faction, first in the form of the Tea Party Caucus and more recently with the rise of the Freedom Caucus, a fiscally and socially conservative group which had an uncompromising approach towards Obama. The Freedom Caucus presented newly elected President Trump with a list of 232 government regulations it wanted to see removed, including economic deregulation as well as removing Obama-era protections.

Coalition of supporters for each party

Specific groups in society tend to support one party more than another. There are both push and pull factors at play, in which a group may be attracted by the policies of one party and/or be repelled by the policies of another.

Voting can be influenced in two ways:
■ party or candidate choice
■ voter turnout

Race

Racial minorities groups are more likely to vote Democrat and white voters are more likely to vote Republican. This is a particularly clear pattern for black voters, with over 90% of black voters typically voting Democrat. This suggests that Obama received a high percentage of the black vote mainly because he is a Democrat and not because he is black. Voter turnout among black voters was at an all-time high in the 2008 and 2012 elections, however. Democrats have supported minority rights much more strongly than Republicans. Donald Trump's campaign was criticised for attacking racial minorities, doing little to attract minority support. Trump surprisingly won 27% of the Hispanic vote in 2016 despite his comments about Hispanics and immigrants.

Religion

Christians, particularly Protestant and evangelical Christians, strongly support the Republican Party. The moral conservatism of the Republican Party, which has been much more resistant to gay rights and abortion, is a major pull factor. Several prominent Republican politicians identify themselves with the **religious right**, such as Sarah Palin, Ben Carson and Ted Cruz.

Some religious groupings, such as Jewish voters, are more likely to vote Democrat. Typically, Jewish voters are supportive of all minority groups and those with low socioeconomic status. This liberal tendency attracts Jewish voters to the liberal moral, economic and welfare policies of the Democrats.

Gender

There is a close split among men and women and their support for each party but men are more likely to vote Republican and women are slightly more likely to vote Democrat. This is a long-term trend. Pull factors include the Democrats' support for women's rights, as well as the prominence of female politicians in the Democratic Party. Trump's comments about women have not helped to switch this balance of support.

Education

There was a clear pattern in 2016, which shows that the more educated a person is the more likely they are to vote Democrat. While Obama managed to secure a majority of the vote in all education groups, Clinton did not. This was partly a response to Trump's populist approach, in which he challenged elites of all types. Higher education levels are associated with liberal values, typically held by the Democratic Party.

Table 33 shows a breakdown of voting preferences in the 2012 and 2016 elections.

Table 33 CNN exit poll figures for social groups in the 2012 and 2016 elections (all figures %)

	2016		2012	
	Clinton	**Trump**	**Obama**	**Romney**
Race				
White	37	58	39	59
Black	88	8	93	6
Hispanic	65	29	71	27
Religion				
Protestant	39	58	42	57
Catholic	45	52	50	48
White evangelical	16	80	21	78
Jewish	71	24	69	30

→

Religious right
A movement of religious leaders, interest groups and politicians who hold a conservative view of Christianity and attempt to promote these views in order to influence both the public and government policy.

Exam tip

The specification asks for students to understand how membership of these groups affected voting in *one recent presidential election*. Make sure you know one election in detail. Knowing how this compares to recent historical trends is also useful.

	2016		2012	
	Clinton	Trump	Obama	Romney
Gender				
Male	41	53	45	52
Female	54	42	55	44
Education				
Postgraduate study	58	37	55	42
College graduate	49	45	47	51
High school or less	45	51	51	48

Interest groups in the USA

Influence, methods and power

Single-interest group

The American Civil Liberties Union

- *What is it?* The ACLU aims to protect constitutional rights, especially 1st Amendment rights. It has a strict view of freedom of expression, for example supporting groups such as the KKK.
- *What methods does it use?* The main methods of the ACLU are legal methods by litigating (initiating court cases) or lobbying the Supreme Court. The ACLU filed an amicus brief in support of the (successful) Westboro Baptist Church in *Snyder* v *Phelps* (2011), which protected the right of the group to hold protests against gay rights at funerals. In 2017, it litigated on behalf of men who were subject to torture methods used by the CIA in detaining terror suspects in the USA under the Bush presidency.
- *How influential is it?* The ACLU has a high degree of influence due to its legal expertise and the high level of rights protection created by the US Constitution. ACLU has successfully won cases which have overturned state and federal law.

Single-interest groups advocate policy surrounding a limited, specific issue.

Professional group

AFL-CIO

- *What is it?* The AFL-CIO is the largest trade union in the United States of America. It has close links with the Democratic Party because of their ideological connections.
- *What methods does it use?* The AFL-CIO uses a variety of methods but commonly uses electioneering to promote Democrat candidates, in terms of publicity, funding and contacting potential voters using its members. It also makes use of lobbying, especially through meetings with senior Democrats. Its president, Richard Trumka, visited the White House six times in Obama's first term.

Professional groups represent the economic interests of their members.

→

■ *How influential is it?* The group has a huge amount of influence given its large membership of 11 million, which can have a major impact on electoral outcomes. In 2012 it registered 450,000 new voters, helping Obama to win the presidency. It is less powerful under Republican control of the presidency and Congress since 2016, although it supports the policy of Trump and not Obama on the Trans Pacific Partnership, which President Trump has rejected.

Policy group

The League of Conservation Voters

■ *What is it?* LCV is a pro-environment group which campaigns on a range of issues such as climate change, protecting parks and public places and opposing the Keystone Pipeline.
■ *What methods does it use?* LCV specialises in affecting electoral outcomes. Its trademark Dirty Dozen is its target list of the most environmentally damaging politicians standing in an election. LCV targets these people through publicity and supporting their opponents.
■ *How influential is it?* LCV has scored some major successes, with 11 of the 12 dirty dozen failing to get elected in 2012. In 2016 it only managed to defeat four of those on its target list (which included President Trump).

Significance, resources, tactics and influence

Significance

Interest groups are significant because they have such a high impact on political processes in the USA. The constitutional and political system encourages high levels of power of interest groups:

■ **Access points.** The separation of powers and federalism create many power centres which groups seek to influence. Failure with one institution does not necessarily mean failure, especially when different parties control different institutions.
■ **Weak parties.** The limited power of party leaders, and limits to party unity, mean that individual politicians are open to persuasion rather than having to follow the party line.
■ **Number and frequency of elections.** The range of elected offices (president, House, Senate and state) and the frequency of congressional elections (every 2 years) give an opportunity for interest groups to exploit this through donations and publicity.
■ **Rights protections.** A powerful Supreme Court coupled with constitutional rights protects basic interest group methods such as freedom of expression (as with the Citizens United case covered above). In addition, some interest group aims are enshrined in the Constitution. This gives success to groups such as The National Rifle Association (2nd Amendment) and The National Association for the Advancement of Colored People (14th Amendment).

Policy groups attempt to influence a whole policy area.

Exam tip

The specification requires students to know at least one single-interest group, professional group and policy group. You could choose other interest groups, such as the National Rifle Association (single-interest group), American Medical Association (professional group) and American Israeli Public Affairs Committee (policy group).

Knowledge check 41

What is meant by an access point for pressure groups?

Resources

Resources are used in order to gain influence. Interest groups with higher resources are likely to be more powerful:

- Members can be used to generate funding through donations and membership fees. In addition, members can be mobilised to contact politicians on key issues or as a show of strength of support.
- Finance is used to donate to election campaigns in the hope of influencing election outcomes or gaining access to elected politicians. It can also be utilised to run publicity campaigns.
- Expertise can be used to be more persuasive in lobbying politicians. Politicians may need the policy expertise of specialist interest groups.
- Contacts within political institutions help to give interest groups access to politicians. This is commonly used by professional lobbyists.

Tactics and influence

Interest groups will use a variety of methods to gain influence:

- Lobbying is used to contact and persuade politicians.
- Electioneering involves any activity, such as donations, publicity and canvassing, which attempts to influence electoral outcome.
- Grassroots activity involves members taking part in political activity through demonstrations or direct action, for example.
- Legal methods are commonly used to influence the courts, especially the Supreme Court.

Interest groups can be a key part of policy creation by developing policy ideas and presenting them to the president or Congress, lobbying relevant politicians for a change in the law. Some interest groups work closely with congressional committees, where policy can be initiated or laws are amended. Table 34 summarises the ways in which pressure groups can influence the three branches of government.

Table 34 How pressure groups influence the executive, legislature and judiciary

Executive/presidency	Legislature/Congress	Judiciary/Supreme Court
- Lobbying through meetings with president, cabinet and EXOP advisors - Electioneering to influence the outcome of the presidential election or gain favour with the successful candidate	- Lobbying through meetings with key political figures or their staff - Focus on relevant committees or chambers, for example the Senate for treaty ratification - Electioneering, particularly making use of short terms	- Litigating by taking a case to court - Lobbying the Court through amicus briefs - Lobbying the Senate to influence Supreme Court nominations

Impact on democracy, including the role of PACs and SuperPACs

Positive impact

Interest groups have a positive impact on democracy:

- They promote participation, allowing people to have a direct influence in the political process. Organising demonstrations or facilitating lobbying campaigns over a specific bill gives individuals a chance to exercise power.
- They represent people by giving a voice to those who may otherwise be overlooked. Interest groups can encourage pluralist democracy by promoting the interests of smaller groups who can be ignored at elections.
- They provide checks on the government, helping to prevent the government from becoming corrupt or self-interested. Interest groups can help to ensure that politicians carry out policy promised.

Negative impact

Interest groups may also limit democracy:

- They use violent or illegal methods which may restrict liberal democracy by restricting the rights of others. They may also break laws passed by democratic procedures which reflect the will of the majority.
- They promote inequality of representation by over representing small but powerful groups. Interest groups may limit the representation of majority views when powerful elites dominate decision making, through their superior resources or contacts.
- They restrict elected government, preventing the legitimate government from carrying out policies.
- Use of finance has become an increasing concern, especially with PAC donations and the rise of SuperPACs since 2010. (See the SuperPACs section, page 67.)

Interpretations and debates of US democracy and participation

Reform of the Electoral College

The advantages and disadvantages of the Electoral College and other aspects of elections such as primaries are addressed above.

There is a longstanding debate about reform, and arguments in favour became stronger with the results of the 2000 and 2016 presidential elections. Possible reforms include:

- the introduction, by constitutional amendment, of a national popular vote system in which the candidate with the most votes in the USA wins
- the removal of faithless electors, either by state law or by constitutional amendment

Reforms have been difficult to establish because of the entrenched constitution. Over-represented states will not agree to remove the Electoral College.

Exam tip

It is useful to go beyond a basic understanding of the concept of democracy, for example by applying different types of democracy. Interest groups might benefit liberal or pluralist democracy by promoting rights, for example, but limit representative democracy by limiting the wishes of the elected president.

Knowledge check 42

What is the difference between a PAC and a SuperPAC?

The role of campaign finance and difficulty in achieving effective reform

Key aspects of the role of campaign finance:

- Political donations are a major source of funding for parties and candidates (with several related concerns outlined above).
- There has been an increase in the role of money in US elections, with greater amounts being spent in election campaigns.
- The regulations on campaign finance have been restricted, which has also increased the importance of money in US elections.
- The creation of SuperPACs has also increased both the role of money and the concerns about that role.
- It must be remembered that money does not necessarily ensure success. First, the highest spender does not necessarily win the election. Second, it may be that one candidate raised the most money because they are the most popular and not the other way around.

Why reform has been difficult to achieve

- Lack of political willingness. Politicians have been reluctant to tighten rules which regulate the money they receive.
- The response of the Supreme Court. Laws have often been undermined because they have been declared unconstitutional, usually in relation to the 1st Amendment (freedom of expression).
- Other loopholes. Wealthy businesses have the resources to find and exploit loopholes, in the form of soft money, which are not easily closed.
- The entrenched constitution. The only effective way to overcome Supreme Court rulings is to amend the Constitution, which has proved impossible in this area. In 2011, Bernie Sanders failed to get his Saving American Democracy amendment passed through Congress.

Comparisons with the UK

The different nature of the party systems

Similarities

- Both countries have two-party systems, with Parliament and Congress being dominated by the two main parties and the executive branch typically controlled by one of the two main parties.
- There is an element of multi-party politics in both countries. Third parties have challenged for control of the executive branch in both countries. In the USA the Libertarian Party (Gary Johnson) and the Green Party (Jill Stein) put forward candidates. The last third-party candidate to win significant votes was Ross Perot in 1992 (18.9% vote) and 1996 (8.4%). In the UK, the Liberal Democrats formed part of the coalition government between 2010 and 2015.

Differences

- The two-party system is weaker in the UK than in the USA. The two main UK parties fall well below the near 100% of seats held by Democrats and Republicans in the US Congress.

- There are stronger regional variations in the UK than in the USA. Democrats and Republicans strongly dominate all states in the USA. In the UK regional governments such as Scotland and Wales are not dominated by the two main parties. The SNP and Plaid Cymru have formed governments in their respective countries since devolution after 1997.

- The two-party system is characterised by a pendulum effect in the UK. One party holds almost all power at one point in time but then power swings to the other party, which takes over in government. In the USA, two parties can be powerful at the same time.

The degree of internal unity within parties

Traditionally, party unity in the USA is much lower than in the UK. The structures of the separation of powers and federalism encourage more fragmented parties with weaker leaders. In the UK the prime minister is typically the leader of the largest party in Parliament and has strong power over this party through patronage. This creates a unified party.

On the other hand, there are some similarities:

- Parties in both countries have a guiding ideology which unites them.
- There are party officials such as leaders and whips who attempt to unify the party.
- Increased partisanship in the USA means that there are similar levels of unity in both countries.
- Major splits do occur in parties in both countries in the form of factions.

The policy profiles of the two main parties in each country

The Labour Party and Democratic Party are associated with left-wing/liberal policies, whereas the Conservative Party and the Republican Party are associated with right-wing/authoritarian policies. The similarities and differences between the two countries are detailed in Table 35.

Debates around campaign finance and party funding

- Campaign finance has been a cause for concern in both countries.
- There is legislation in place which regulates campaign finance such as FECA and BCRA in the USA and the Political Parties, Elections and Referendums Act 2000 (PPERA) in the UK, which required all parties to register with the Electoral Commission and put controls on donations.
- Maximum expenditure limits no longer apply in practice in the USA whereas they do in the UK. The refusal of presidential candidates to take federal funding and the creation of SuperPACs mean that regulations are very limited in the USA.

Knowledge check 43

What are the names of the main pieces of legislation which regulate campaign finance in the UK and USA?

....

Table 35 Similarities and differences between UK and US political parties

Policy	Similarities	However...
Social and moral	Labour and the Democrats have been at the forefront of developments in the protection of rights such as the Civil Rights Act in the USA and the Human Rights Act in the UK The right-wing parties in each country have opposed or not committed themselves to the enhancement of such rights	In the UK it was Cameron's Conservative government which legalised gay marriage (although the party was divided on the issue)
Welfare and social justice	Labour and Democrats hold similar views, supporting increased government intervention to help those with lower socioeconomic status. These two parties call for protections in welfare and have pushed for the introduction of, and increase in, the national minimum wage, for example Conservatives and Republicans have called for cuts in these areas	The Conservative Party is much less right wing than the Republican Party on many welfare issues, partly because the USA as a whole is more right wing in this area Conservative prime ministers have been committed to keeping the NHS as a government-run health service free at the point of use. This is more left wing than the approach taken by even the Democratic Party in the USA
Economic	The Conservative and Republican parties have stressed the importance of individual freedom, with an attempt to reduce the role of government in the economy (and welfare) with fewer regulations, lower expenditure and lower taxation These two parties are associated with tax cuts for the wealthy	Both moderate Democrats and New Labour have adopted policies more in line with centre-ground/right-wing thinking. Blair's Labour did not increase the higher rate of income tax and abandoned plans to renationalise industry. Democrats have been accused of doing too little to regulate banking In both countries there is a struggle between moderate and more left-wing factions

The relative power, methods and influence of pressure groups

Methods

- While pressure groups use similar methods, they are used differently in each country because of the different structures of the political system.
- There is a greater use of litigation in the USA because of the power of the Supreme Court.
- The existence of insiders and outsiders in the UK might deter some pressure groups from lobbying, turning to demonstrations and direct action instead. In the USA, on the other hand, access points encourage a greater level of lobbying by all groups.

Power and influence

It can be argued that, pressure groups exert more influence in the USA.

- There are more access points in the USA. The fusion of powers means that the government dominates Parliament in the UK. The government is the only significant access point for pressure groups, with some failing due to conflicting ideological views with those in power.
- The greater number of elections and their cost in the USA mean that pressure groups play a bigger role in electoral outcomes than in the UK. Political parties in the UK have greater control over their own candidates and the flow of money.
- The existence of weaker parties in the USA suggests that interest groups can be more influential over political processes by influencing individual politicians. UK politicians are more controlled by party leaders than those in the USA.

Rational, cultural and structural approaches

The actions of pressure groups and parties can be seen as culturally driven because there is a shared value within each group. Members of trade unions in the USA (AFL-CIO) and in the UK (TUC) work together to pursue policy goals. Political parties have unity, with evidence that politicians sometimes work towards the dominant cultural value of their party rather than their own personal interest or view. David Cameron allowed an EU referendum despite his personal support of the EU because of the strong views in his own party. Hillary Clinton adjusted her position on issues such as the Keystone Pipeline, adopting the dominant party view.

On the other hand, a lack of party unity can be explained using the rational approach. Politicians may be acting selfishly by promoting their own views and not the views of the party, because it is what they believe in. This is arguably more prevalent in the USA with weaker parties, suggesting that the actions of US politicians can more easily be described as rational in motivation, compared to the UK. In voting for a bill, a US or UK politician may be acting rationally by following constituency views and attempting to get re-elected, rather than following the cultural views of their party.

The structural approach is also important in understanding similarities and differences between the two countries. In particular, it can explain differences in the level of power of parties or pressure groups in each country. US pressure groups have greater influence because of structural differences such as the separation of powers in the USA and the fusion of powers in the UK. In addition, parties may be weaker in the UK because of the same constitutional structures.

Summary

- Presidential elections make use of the Electoral College rather than a national popular vote.
- There are a series of other stages before the presidential vote, covering invisible primaries, primaries and national party conventions.
- Campaign finance and its regulation is a major issue in US elections.
- SuperPACs in the USA have a significant impact on US elections.
- There are two main US parties, Democrats and Republicans, each with its own factions and coalition of supporters.
- Interest groups play a major role in the US system, particularly due to constitutional factors, which promotes their power.
- Students are required to have an awareness of at least one single-interest group, one policy group and one professional group.

Questions & Answers

How to approach the Paper 3 exam

A-level Paper 3, Comparative US Politics, requires you to answer questions on the politics of the United States of America as well as comparative questions in which you compare and contrast the UK and US political systems. It is important that you check the Edexcel website for the latest specification material and any updates to the content or assessment.

The key features of the paper

- The written examination is a 2-hour paper.
- It is worth one-third of your A-level marks.
- The paper is worth 84 marks in total.

The paper has three sections:

Section A

- You will answer one 12-mark question from a choice of two comparing US and UK politics.
- There are up to 6 marks for AO1 and 6 marks for AO2 (see below for an outline of assessment objectives).
- All questions in this section will ask you to 'examine'.
- Suggested approach — you will successfully examine if you:
  - compare the two countries directly in relation to the key word(s) of the question
  - cover three or four points/paragraphs
  - explain each idea using comparisons to draw out differences and similarities (take care to answer the question, some will require only similarities or differences and others may require both)
  - include contemporary evidence *and* relate it to the question asked

Section B

- You will answer one compulsory 12-mark question comparing the USA and the UK *and* applying one or more of the three main comparative theories (rational, cultural and structural).
- There are up to 6 marks for AO1 and 6 marks for AO2.
- All questions will ask you to 'analyse'.
- This has a similar requirement and approach to Section A questions except that you are required to apply one or more of the three comparative theories in order to gain marks on AO2.

Section C

- You will answer two 30-mark questions from a choice of three, focused on US politics only.
- There are up to 10 marks for each of AO1, AO2 and AO3.
- All questions will ask you to 'evaluate'.
- You can then evaluate by making judgements about the strengths of certain ideas or arguments. It is important to do this throughout your answer.
- A useful approach is to write an introduction, followed by a series of arguments and counter-arguments or arguments and evaluation of each argument, followed by a conclusion.

Assessment objectives (AOs)

There are three AOs, with marks being awarded for:

- **AO1 Knowledge and understanding.** This requires you to show an awareness of the key political ideas, facts and processes. This includes an awareness of contemporary evidence.
- **AO2 Analysis.** This requires you to apply your knowledge to the key word(s) of the question, for example by making connections, showing an awareness of relevant similarities or differences and showing an understanding of the changing nature of political systems. Remember that in Section B comparative questions this command requires you to apply one or more comparative theories.
- **AO3 Evaluation.** This requires you to develop arguments, make judgements, especially about the strength of arguments, and come to conclusions. It applies to 30-mark questions only, for this paper.

The exam questions in this Guide

This Guide includes examination-style questions designed to be a key learning, revision and exam preparation resource. Each question is followed by a sample student answer. These are accompanied by an examiner commentary (indicated by the icon **e**), as well as the total number of marks awarded. Use the commentaries to help improve your own question technique and knowledge.

Immediately below each question are some tips (indicated by the icon **e**) on how to approach your answer.

■ Section A questions

US Constitution

Examine the similarities in the way that 'checks and balances' operates in the USA and UK.

(12 marks)

(e) This question requires you to have a good understanding of the definition of 'checks and balances' and how this works in reality rather than in theory — this is how it 'operates'. You are only looking for *similarities*; do not do differences! Once you have identified a similarity, for example that the power of the purse rests with the lower house in both countries, you must explain how this similarity works in reality and begin to think about the extent of the similarity.

Student answer

One similarity is the power of the legislative branches to declare war. In the USA, this has been an enumerated power of Congress since the ratification of the Constitution in 1789. The UK Parliament gained this power in 2007 when Brown gave this traditionally prerogative power to Parliament. (a) In both countries this power has operated in such a way as to prevent the executive branch from exercising complete control over foreign policy. Recently, both the US Congress and the UK Parliament were able to use this power to prevent President Obama and Prime Minister Cameron from taking military action in Syria. This has allowed both legislatures to act as an effective check on the executive branch, which prevents the tyranny of either the president or the prime minister in this policy. (b)

(e) The student immediately demonstrates a similarity in the opening line (there is no need to paraphrase the question!), (a) using precise political vocabulary ('enumerated', 'prerogative') and showing detailed examples about this power. (b) The second half focuses on the AO2 skill of analysis, explaining the impact of this check and giving a recent, comparable example. In using language such as 'effective', and explaining the use of this word, this is a high-level answer which fully addresses the question.

Another similarity is the role of the judiciary as an independent check on the elected branches. Life tenure, guaranteed funds and the power of judicial review allow both judiciaries confidence when challenging the government. In thwarting the UK government's claim that it could trigger Brexit without Parliament, and Obama's DAPA and DACA immigration reform, the Supreme Courts demonstrated that they can protect the constitutions of their respective countries against the will of the elected government. (c) This is crucial in preventing the democracy of each country succumbing to the tyranny of the majority.

(e) The student continues to demonstrate detailed knowledge of theory and examples, which fulfils the AO1 criteria. (c) Importantly, however, they explain how this similarity works in operation, which directly addresses the question, moving away from simplistic description into AO2 analysis.

While in these landmark cases the governments were effectively challenged, the reality is often that the government of both countries can exercise considerably greater power than the judiciary, albeit for different reasons. d In the USA, the Supreme Court can only be formally overruled with a constitutional amendment, but in practice relies on the government to enforce its will. In the UK, the court is arguably weaker than this, taking its basis from statute law and therefore its existence is only guaranteed by Parliament. In both cases, these weaknesses allow for the executive to have greater dominance within their systems than checks and balances should allow for.

e While this paragraph lacks examples, this is to be expected given its length and the time constraints. d Impressively, the student has identified a similarity while demonstrating judgement about this similarity. They continue to show the impact of this check and balance *in operation*, which is crucial for AO2.

The checks and balances of both countries also allow for the removal of the executive by the legislature. e In the UK, since the Fixed Term Parliaments Act 2011, a vote of no confidence gives the government 14 days to gain the confidence of the House of Commons or face election, handing the choice effectively to the electorate. While different in practice, the USA has a similar check allowing Congress to impeach the president. Parliament does have greater freedom in the use of this power, not restrained by a codified constitution, and has exercised it more frequently, lastly in 1979. Nonetheless, the threat of impeachment should prevent a tyrannous executive, therefore effectively allowing for the same check in both countries. f

e d This final paragraph shows a wealth of contextual and up-to-date knowledge but ensures that the focus remains on the operation of checks and balances. f The final sentence is a great example of judgement to *show* comparison between the two countries, rather than simply describing both and expecting the examiner to work out the similarities.

e **12/12 marks awarded.** This is a Level 4 answer with the student demonstrating accurate theory and examples throughout, all of which are directly relevant to this specific question (AO1). The student is keenly focused on the question. They address AO2 skills thoroughly, showing consistent analysis in each paragraph and making good judgements about these similarities. The balanced use of the judiciary over two paragraphs is especially impressive and demonstrates logical reasoning.

US Congress

Examine the extent to which Parliament and Congress are able to check the executive branch.

(12 marks)

e This question requires you to directly compare the ability of Parliament and Congress to restrict the executive (government and president). As an 'extent' question, you have to consider how effective these checks are by considering different ways in which Parliament and Congress can provide checks. It is extremely useful to show an awareness of how the Constitution makes Congress more effective than Parliament.

Student answer

Congress is more able to provide significant checks on the executive than Parliament due to the level of separation of powers and checks and balances in the two countries. In the UK the parliamentary system gives the government (and usually one party) a majority of seats in the Commons and allows the executive to have a huge amount of patronage power over MPs. In the USA the separation of powers means that the president may not have a congressional majority and he does not have the ability to influence Congress through patronage. **a** This means that Congress is far more likely to be willing to provide checks on the executive. This can be seen in the relative success of the executive's legislative proposals with greater scrutiny and rejection in the USA. UK governments, even the coalition, successfully pass all their bills. In the USA President Trump was unable to pass legislation to repeal Obamacare despite a Republican majority, suggesting much stronger checks. **b**

e This is a strong paragraph, which is well focused on the question. It compares throughout, **a** showing a central difference between the two systems and **b** presenting evidence from both countries.

In addition, the USA has two powerful chambers, both of which can provide extensive scrutiny. Arguably the Lords provide a much weaker level of checks than the Senate. Lords are unable to reject government bills, unlike the Senate, for example. The Senate also has specific scrutiny powers such as ratifying treaties and presidential appointments, which the Lords do not. For this reason, it is unlikely that UK governments would fail to secure treaties in the way that Obama did when the Senate failed to ratify the disability treaty or Clinton failing to get a chemical weapons treaty ratified. **c**

e This paragraph adds another reason why Congress provides more effective checks. It is still a strong paragraph, although it is shorter. **c** It provides evidence from the USA but not the UK. It does try to compare the US example with the UK situation, however.

On the other hand, Parliament can and does provide strong checks through select committees, votes of no confidence (which do not exist in the USA) and votes on legislation. This suggests that both legislatures provide strong checks. Recent Conservative governments have been defeated on the initial plan to bomb Syria as well as aiming to further liberalise Sunday trading laws. **d** The theory of the imperial presidency may even suggest that the checks provided by Congress are lower with the president evading checks through the use of executive orders and executive agreements. President Obama bypassed Congress by signing an order to enforce parts of the Dream Act and made deals with many countries that were not subject to a Senate vote (such as Cuba, China and Iran). **e**

e This section continues to compare the two countries directly throughout, increasing its strength in AO2, and this time providing the other side of the argument. This is important because the question asks for a judgement of extent. The answer has a real strength in showing off a range of detailed contemporary examples for **d** the UK *and* **e** the USA.

> The extent to which checks are effective partly depends on the nature of party majorities, however. If a president has a majority then Congress might provide weaker checks. This majority along with strong public support for Bush after 9/11 meant that Congress was accused of failing to provide adequate checks on a dominant president. In the UK governments with low or no majorities may be checked more effectively. This was part of the reason why Theresa May called for an early election, due to her low parliamentary majority.

e This paragraph makes an all-important point about politics — it is a changing situation, in which the level of checks depends on other factors. In this case the student makes a strong argument about the nature of government majorities.

e **12/12 marks awarded.** This is clearly a Level 4 answer. It has fully accurate knowledge, including evidence of the ways in which legislatures provide checks (AO1). This student could not be expected to cover more ground in the time available. It also has consistent comparative analysis, carefully comparing in every paragraph and making good judgements about the extent of checks (AO2). The structure of the answer is very strong, with two paragraphs arguing that Congress is more able to check, one arguing that Parliament is stronger and a final paragraph covering the idea that it depends on context.

US presidency

Examine the ability of the prime minister and president to achieve their policy aims.

(12 marks)

e The focus of this question is the ability 'to achieve…policy aims'. This means you must be able to show how the powers that each executive has, formal or informal, can help them to get their way. As this is an 'examine' question, you are required to identify any similarities or differences in their ability. It would be more useful to compare the executives within each paragraph, rather than simply describing their powers independently.

Student answer

> The US president, being directly elected, holds an individual mandate for policies on which he campaigned. Obama's key pledge for healthcare reform arguably gave him a mandate to carry out Obamacare as a policy once he was elected. While this policy was considerably amended in Congress, ultimately, it was difficult for them to reject without potentially facing a backlash from the public, which enables the president some power over issues he campaigned on.

The UK prime minister, by comparison, has far greater power to force through issues they campaigned upon provided they included them in their manifesto due to the Salisbury Convention. This ensures that their passage cannot be rejected by Parliament as the government effectively has a mandate from the people for these policies.

ⓔ This is a good opening paragraph, showing clear comparison of a similar point. The point about the Salisbury Convention is not as closely tied to the question as it does not explicitly refer to the prime minister but it does have relevance.

The UK prime minister clearly has greater ability to force new policies through Parliament, however. Winning the election not only provides them with a doctor's mandate, it also delivers a majority in the House of Commons. With fused power of the executive and legislature, this allows the prime minister to effectively force through legislation not in their manifesto, especially with the use of the whips. The president cannot control Congress so closely. Even if his party controls both houses, he is not in charge of them and so cannot force through policy.

ⓔ This paragraph shows good theoretical detail, although an example would be illustrative here. It is well written, if unbalanced in the comparison. The section on the USA relies more on AO1 rather than explaining *why* the president lacks this control. The UK section is much more sound.

Both executives annually lay out their policy priorities for the coming year and this allows them some power to direct policy. The president outlines his wishes at the State of the Union and it is convention that bills with presidential support should pass through Congress, even though they may get amended along the way. However, this has not always proved effective and Obama failed to get immigration reform or gun control passed. The Queen's Speech in the UK is written by the government and so it not only publicises the policy priorities for the coming year, it should also ensure support for them with the government's majority.

ⓔ This is a stronger paragraph, now including a worked example, although it is not explicit as to why this example is included. The student is still using the government and PM interchangeably and while there is a clear link they should try to show awareness of the distinction between the PM and the government.

While the UK prime minister holds more power within the legislature in order to pass their policy, the president can use other means to achieve his aims. Executive orders allow for a president to somewhat circumvent Congress. While they are not allowed to be new law, they have the effect of law and many presidents have used them to achieve a difficult policy goal, as Obama did with immigration. The president therefore has a broader range of ways to endeavour to achieve his policy aims, perhaps because it is more difficult through Congress. While the UK prime minister has fewer, they can be more assured of their success due to their majority.

e This is a nicely analytical paragraph, which brings out some good themes. It does read a little like a conclusion, which is not required for this type of question, but the judgement is good for AO2 marks. Again, the example could be developed but the comparison is strong.

e **10/12 marks awarded.** This is a sound answer which manages to just reach Level 4. It shows accurate knowledge and good comparisons between the two countries, which addresses AO1 skills. While examples and analysis could stand for development, this is a good attempt in the limited time of an examination. The student has demonstrated clear judgement throughout, making consistent comparisons (AO2) made on the basis of sound reasoning.

US Supreme Court and civil rights

Examine the extent of independence of the UK and US Supreme Courts. (12 marks)

e The focus of this question is the 'extent'; do not fall into the trap of simply describing theoretical ways in which independence is guaranteed. It is important to understand the difference between independence and neutrality — this question only deals with independence. As this is a comparative question, you must compare how similar (or different) methods of ensuring independence are actually successful in either country.

> **Student answer**
>
> Separation of powers is important to ensuring independence of the judiciary. The Supreme Court in the USA has its independence guaranteed by being outlined in the Constitution as separate from the presidency and Congress. In the UK, this is not as clear. The Supreme Court has existed as an independent body since 2009, however it only exists because of the Constitutional Reform Act (CRA) 2005. As a law of Parliament, this could be revoked as Parliament is sovereign. As the US Constitution itself is sovereign, it seems that the US Supreme Court holds greater independence as it does not have to be concerned over its existence.

e This is a sound paragraph that shows reasonable understanding of the theory and examples relevant to the question. It is quite descriptive, although the student does briefly explain *why* separation of powers protects independence towards the end. It also draws comparison and makes a basic judgement at the end.

> The justices in the UK Court hold more independence than those in the USA. This is because they are appointed by the Judicial Appointments Commission which is politically independent since the CRA 2005. This means that justices are selected by experts rather than politicians and therefore do not owe politicians anything. a In the USA, the justices are nominated by the president and appointed by Congress. Obama nominated Sotomayor, who was confirmed by a Democratic-dominated Senate. This means not only are politicians involved, but that they will choose judges based on other factors than their experience and suitability, such as ideology.

e This is a clearly defined separate point with a well-identified if not explained example. It does describe the two systems but it would be good to have more explicit comparisons drawn. **a** The language is also not as refined as a top-grade answer.

> Independence in both countries is equally guaranteed by the independent payment of justices. This means that politicians cannot alter their pay if they do not like what the justices are ruling. In the USA, their pay is protected by the Constitution whereas in the UK their pay comes from a Consolidated Fund. In both cases this is aimed to ensure that judges cannot effectively be made to act on behalf of the government by threatening their pay.

e This is the weakest of the paragraphs — accurate but descriptive and with limited AO2 analysis. The length of a paragraph does not always guarantee good marks but invariably shorter paragraphs are likely to rely on description (AO1) over analysis (AO2).

> Both countries are also similar in their protection of independence through life tenure. In the USA, the only way a justice can be removed is through impeachment, but otherwise there are no limits provided they are acting in 'good behaviour'. In the UK, a judge can only be removed for being corrupt, although there is also an upper age limit of 75, which there is not in the USA. By guaranteeing their tenure, this should ensure that justices' jobs cannot be threatened by the government and therefore they can act in accordance with the law rather than simply as the government wants them to.

e This is a stronger paragraph than the preceding one, although it effectively makes the same point using a different example. Students should be wary of this as it will restrict the amount of marks they will gain.

e **8/12 marks awarded.** This is a sound Level 3 answer. It demonstrates sound theoretical knowledge of the two systems (AO1). It is very formulaic in the way it is written, which is a matter of nuance; however, to gain top marks the way an analysis is written is important. The comparative analysis is well identified but not always developed, lacking the consistency necessary for Level 4 (AO2). The language and logic here is more basic than some of the higher-level answers. Nonetheless it does address the question, providing knowledge, evidence and some analysis.

US democracy and participation

Examine the extent to which campaign finance regulations have been effective in the UK and USA.

(12 marks)

e Comparing campaign finance regulations can be approached by looking at what the legislation is trying to achieve. For example, in both countries the legislation aims to limit expenditure, limit the influence of major donors and ensure transparency. It is better to compare the US and UK systems directly in each paragraph, by writing a paragraph on each of these areas.

Student answer

In both the USA and the UK campaign finance regulation has been effective with extensive legislation regulating money in elections. **a** This is effective in the sense that it is tackling some of the major concerns including the inequality of spending between the main parties/candidates and the excessive influence of donors. In the UK the Political Parties, Elections and Referendums Act 2000 (PPERA) limits donations and expenditure. In 2015 parties were limited to £19.5m and candidates could only spend £30,000 in their constituency. In the USA the main legislation (FECA and McCain–Feingold) have limited expenditure and donations. All of this has helped to limit the influence of money in US and UK elections, particularly in terms of equality of spending. The two main parties or candidates often spend similar amounts of money, allowing for a fair election.

e This is a good opening paragraph for a Section A comparative question. **a** It goes straight to the key point, without an introduction, giving the student more time to explore more key points. It also shows a good understanding of the key word of the question by explaining what effective means in the context of this question.

Campaign finance regulation appears to be much more effective in the UK, however. The spending and donation limits are much lower, limiting the influence of money to a greater extent. In addition, campaign finance regulation has largely failed in the USA, making the regulations meaningless. Unlike in the UK, there is no effective spending limit on presidential candidates because they can only apply when the candidate takes federal funding, which they no longer need to. Since George Bush refused federal funding in 2000 and both Obama and Romney followed this in 2012, restrictions have been irrelevant. This suggests that regulations fail to work to a greater extent in the USA.

e This is a strong paragraph, which compares by showing a key difference between the two countries. It continues to compare throughout the paragraph.

Another central difference is the existence in the USA of a written codified constitution with 1st Amendment rights to free speech, which does not exist to the same extent in the UK. **b** This has been used to limit campaign finance regulation in the USA with a series of Supreme Court rulings such as *Citizens United* v *FEC*. SuperPACs can now take unlimited donations and campaign on behalf of parties or candidates, particularly using advertising. The rules regulating advertising, the media and donations in the UK are much stricter, limiting the extent to which money is influential. **c** In 2017 it was discovered that there were finance irregularities in some UK constituency expenditure for several Conservative MPs. This might suggest that the UK suffers from the same problems as the USA where rules can be avoided. **e** On the other hand, the discovery of these issues and the subsequent legal action again suggest stronger regulation in the UK with no possibility of the regulations being challenged as unconstitutional. **d**

ⓔ This paragraph adopts a useful structure by **ⓑ** directly comparing in the opening line, **ⓒ** explaining the differences with ongoing comparison and **ⓓ** providing comparative evidence.

> Supporters of elite theories might see little difference between the two countries with finance regulations failing in both. They might argue that elite interests exert huge influence in both countries. **ⓔ** Political parties in the USA and UK both depend on funding, especially from business, in order to run successful electoral campaigns. Even though the level of expenditure is much lower in the UK, if parties need corporate money then they may have undue influence. The *Daily Telegraph*'s exposure of the Tory Diners Club, in which major donors were given access to politicians, including the PM, suggests a degree of elitism in the UK. Many members of Congress are seen as captives of big business, with politicians such as Democrat Senator Harry Reid promoting the interests of the gambling industry, which donates to his Nevada campaign. Regulations have therefore failed in one of their aims to limit the influence of donors.

ⓔ This is an important paragraph because it provides an alternative perspective. The question is not just asking for similarities or differences but extent. **ⓔ** By applying elite theory the student shows how the two countries might be similar despite the differences outlined in the previous two paragraphs.

ⓔ **12/12 marks awarded.** This is a Level 4 answer, which shows a very good awareness of the main regulations in each country and the evidence of spending in elections (AO1). The response consistently compares when judging the extent of similarities and differences, again suggesting a Level 4 answer. It makes very good use of the extent to which the two countries are similar and different in order to explain the extent to which finance regulations work (AO2).

■ Section B questions

US Constitution

Analyse the extent of flexibility in the UK and US constitutions.　　　　(12 marks)

In your answer you must consider the relevance of a least one comparative theory.

ⓔ In an 'analyse' question, you are required to use one of the comparative theories (rational, cultural, structural) in order to gain top marks. This question is an 'extent' question and therefore you are looking at both sides, flexible and not flexible. Once you have identified the similarities or differences, which are best given a paragraph each, you must explain the existence of one of these by using a theory. The most natural one for this question would be structural.

Student answer

The US Constitution is viewed as more rigid than the UK's due to the entrenched and codified nature of the document. Being codified in one document, the US Constitution very clearly lays out the power of each branch of government and the rights of citizens, making it difficult for the government to infringe upon these rights. While the US Government may view Guantanamo Bay as necessary for national security, in 2004 the government was forced to make concessions to detainees due to a Supreme Court case. This demonstrates the rigidity of the Constitution, preventing the elected government from acting as it wishes.

ⓔ This is a brilliant opening paragraph. The political language demonstrates keen understanding while the knowledge is detailed and specific. Although it is focused only on the USA, the student goes on to draw comparison in the next paragraph, allowing greater space for detailed analysis. Importantly, they are reviewing 'the extent' of flexibility, not just describing.

Comparatively, the UK Constitution is viewed as hugely flexible, being uncodified and unentrenched. Unlike in the USA, sovereignty does not rest in the constitution but in Parliament, allowing it the power to effectively alter the UK Constitution as it sees fit. The Fixed Term Parliaments Act 2011 changed the very nature of Parliament in the UK and yet was passed by a simple Act of Parliament which requires just a majority vote, effectively allowing the elected government to act as it wishes. This difference can be explained culturally, as the UK has never had a codified constitution, nor had any event of massive political upheaval to warrant one. The uncodified and flexible nature of the constitution is therefore culturally accepted, compared to the USA where protections against a potentially tyrannous government are viewed as a cultural necessity.

ⓔ Clear comparisons to the USA are drawn throughout this paragraph. The student also begins to draw in the comparative theories — you must mention at least one of rational, cultural or structural, and picking the most relevant theory is a skill in itself. Crucially, this candidate uses the theory to *explain* why these constitutions have differing flexibility, key for AO2.

Despite this, the US Constitution does have some flexibility. Article V of the Constitution allows for amendments, of which there have been 27, but perhaps more frequently Supreme Court rulings offer interpretive amendments to the Constitution. *Obergefell* v *Hodges* in 2015 effectively legalised gay marriage across all 50 states despite there being no explicit mention of this in the Constitution. This demonstrates a similar level of flexibility to the UK Constitution, which added the Marriage (Same Sex) Couples Act in 2013. This similarity is best explained structurally, reviewing where power lies. The US Constitution allows for the power of the Supreme Court to carry out such amendments within the document itself. In the UK, the nature of parliamentary democracy ensures the sovereignty of Parliament to carry out constitutional amendments. In both cases, this allows for constitutional evolution and flexibility.

e This paragraph demonstrates good judgement — the student is showing that this is not simply a case of US rigidity versus UK flexibility, and that the reality is somewhat more nuanced. They have also used a clever example as it is directly comparable between the two countries. The student has introduced a second comparative theory, and while this is not required, it is well explained.

Indeed, it could be argued that this in fact allows for too much flexibility within the UK Constitution. In the USA, at least constitutional changes require a supermajority agreement or are undertaken by the independent judiciary. In the UK, allowing Parliament such power means that the constitution can effectively be changed on a whim — while the Fixed Term Parliaments Act was introduced in 2011, it has already been undermined by the calling of a snap election in 2017. This level of flexibility potentially affords too much power to the UK government.

e Again, the level of judgement is clear from the outset of this paragraph and continues throughout, constantly comparing. It shows clear understanding of the amendment processes and is right up to date.

e **12/12 marks awarded.** This is a Level 4 answer. The student has demonstrated accurate theoretical and contextual knowledge throughout and shows a complete understanding of comparative theories in explaining these differences (AO1), allowing them to move beyond Level 3. They have avoided simple description of both systems, instead drawing comparisons and showing thoughtful and relevant judgement throughout that is closely focused on the question asked (AO2).

e In this question you are only being asked to look at differences between Congress and Parliament. Your answer could pick three or four differences and, for each one, explain how one of the three comparative theories can explain what is the cause of that difference.

US Congress

Analyse the differences in the ability of Congress and Parliament to provide adequate representation.

(12 marks)

In your answer you must consider the relevance of a least one comparative theory.

Student answer

Both Congress and Parliament are not very representative due to the first-past-the-post voting system. In both countries there are single-member constituencies in which the winner takes all. Only a simple majority of votes is needed to win. In both countries there are safe seats and disproportionality. Third parties do not do very well and if a voter votes for them they may not win. In the UK Parliament smaller parties such as the Liberal Democrats and UKIP are under-represented. FPTP means that third parties do not usually exist in the USA with even lower levels of representation. **a** In both countries there is a lack of representation, therefore.

e This paragraph compares the two countries and directly addresses the question of representation with a point about the voting system. Overall it could be much stronger, however. First, it does not make use of any of the three comparative theories, which is an absolute requirement for Section B compulsory comparative questions. It is better to include discussion of a theory in each paragraph. Second, it does not focus on the question, which asks for difference — this paragraph is mainly focused on similarities and explaining how first past the post works, only directly answering the question at one point **a**.

Parliament is far less representative due to the unelected Lords compared to the elected Senate. The Lords are not accountable to the public and do not have to respond to public opinion. Senators are very concerned with public opinion, especially as their term develops. The structural theory explains a key difference. Elections provide a structure in the USA which forces politicians to respond to public opinion but this structure does not exist for the Lords. This can be seen in the Lords' attitude to the EU when they rejected the 'take it or leave it' Brexit vote put to them in 2016, despite the referendum result. Senators such as John McCain have been known to change their voting behaviour to respond more to constituents in an election year. **b**

e This paragraph compares the two countries and makes use of a comparative theory. It also presents evidence, with some detail. This makes it much stronger than the previous paragraph. **b** The evidence could be better linked to the question. The EU example is highly questionable given that the Lords backed down on the issue, partly in recognition of their unelected nature. The McCain example is an interesting one, in which the student could have explained more about what this says regarding representation.

> Parliament is less representative than Congress in terms of race, gender and class. c Congress has more black and female politicians than Parliament, which means that Parliament does not look like Britain. d In addition, increased partisanship means that Congress has become less representative because politicians respond to the party and not the public. e This suggests that a cultural approach can explain a difference. US parties have become more partisan. In Parliament, MPs may rebel from the party culture due to constituency needs, as can be seen with Brexit.

e This is a weaker paragraph, which would benefit from focusing on one main idea and developing it further. c The section begins with a direct and relevant comparison — a good approach. d The point about female and black politicians is not very clear, with limited specific evidence. What is important is not the number but the percentage of, say, racial minority members compared to the percentage in the country as a whole. e The paragraph then moves on to another point about partisanship and makes use of a comparative theory (cultural). The exact differences between the two countries are unclear (it is usually argued that party loyalty is higher in the UK than in the USA). This idea could be unpacked with further evidence *and* related to representation even more.

e **6/12 marks awarded.** This is a weaker answer, which reaches Level 2. While some of the knowledge and understanding is superficial (Level 1), overall the answer does enough to demonstrate some accurate knowledge and understanding of the processes relating to representation. It also applies comparative theory in two paragraphs, although it could do so with more explanation (AO2). Higher marks could be gained through more consistent and detailed application of comparative theory to help it go beyond Level 2, where the comparison can be described as emerging, rather than mostly focused (Level 3). A higher level could be reached with more detailed and accurate use of evidence, focusing on the question (differences) in every paragraph *and* dealing with just one idea in each paragraph, to allow for development and clarity.

US presidency

Analyse the extent to which the US president and the UK prime minister control their cabinet.

(12 marks)

In your answer you must consider the relevance of a least one comparative theory.

e As an 'extent' question, this is requiring you to look both positively and negatively. This means you are not just saying that they both control their cabinet but which one controls their cabinet more and why. The factors that allow for control over the cabinet can be broken down and you should compare the two countries within one paragraph for each. Remember to explain at least one of the similarities or differences using a comparative theory.

Student answer

As the head of the cabinet, both the prime minister and president appear to have similar control. They both choose the members of their cabinet. In the UK, cabinet members usually come from Parliament, such as Justine Greening who is an MP. In the US, cabinet members are not drawn from Congress but are confirmed by them. In this way, the prime minister has more control a as there are no checks on his or her appointment to cabinet, whereas the president must ensure his appointments will be ratified.

e This paragraph does address the question, and focuses on differences, but the examples and theory are underdeveloped. The student does not explain on what basis each executive may make their choice, which would help to explain the level of control they have. **a** The student has used words from the question but not explained them very well, instead relying on description.

The cabinets of each country are quite different in operation and this affects the control the executive can have. The UK cabinet is a collective body meaning that ministers are bound by collective responsibility and ministers going against this should resign. In the USA, the cabinet is only advisory with all power being vested in 'a president'. This means that cabinet members can speak out against the president, as former Defense Secretary Hagel did over Guantanamo Bay. These structural differences mean that the prime minister is far more able to control the cabinet than the president.

e This is an improvement on the first paragraph but still overly descriptive (AO1), rather than analytical (AO2). The student shows knowledge of the power of cabinet but does not effectively show how they have reached the analysis made in their final sentence. There is a hint of understanding of comparative theories here but it does not demonstrate understanding of the theory.

There have been cases, however, where a lack of control over the cabinet has been far more evident, and concerning, in the UK. Thatcher was ultimately removed by her cabinet, demonstrating a lack of control over it. The US president would be unlikely to face such circumstances as the lack of power based within the cabinet means he is more able to hire and fire at will without repercussions.

e At only three sentences, this paragraph is almost exclusively AO1 knowledge and does not show how the UK prime minister failed to control her cabinet; rather it simply states that the cabinet removed her. It is also somewhat repetitious of the first paragraph.

> The president can use executive orders to guide the actions of cabinet departments, therefore attempting to control his cabinet secretaries. While these do not have the force of law, they do tell departments how he wishes laws to be carried out. Comparatively, the UK PM looks to direct cabinet more subtly — Blair had his 'sofa cabinet', for example. This could be explained rationally as the PM knows the cabinet has the power to unseat them and therefore must be more wary of cabinet whereas the US president has a direct mandate from the people and can therefore act more freely and give directions to his cabinet more openly.

e This is a far stronger paragraph but not enough to save the whole essay. It is more detailed in both theoretical knowledge and examples and shows a better link to the comparative theories. Had the other paragraphs been like this, the essay could have achieved more highly.

e **7/12 marks awarded.** This is low Level 3 answer. The student has a reasonable identification of knowledge and examples but does not always deploy them effectively, relying on lengthy description over analysis (AO1). The references to comparative theories need to show greater understanding. The student has mostly selected appropriate knowledge but in order to advance must ensure a closer focus on the question, which is about executive control, not cabinet power. The paragraphs are too inconsistent in their analysis (AO2) to move beyond low Level 3.

US Supreme Court and civil rights

Analyse the effectiveness of the UK and US Supreme Courts at protecting civil rights.

(12 marks)

In your answer you must consider the relevance of a least one comparative theory.

e This is an 'effectiveness' question and you could be tripped up if you just look at what they are supposed to do in theory. To be 'effective', the Supreme Courts must actually protect rights in reality too. This means you might begin to talk about the sovereignty of Parliament in the UK undermining the Supreme Court, whereas the sovereignty of the US Constitution aids the Supreme Court.

Student answer

The Supreme Court of both countries can use judicial review to protect civil rights. This means they can take a court case to decide whether the government has taken away someone's rights. The UK Supreme Court recently heard a case regarding whether women in Northern Ireland were allowed abortions on the NHS. In America, the Supreme Court decided that Texas could not close down abortion clinics. In both cases the rights of women to abortion were protected.

e This is a basic, and at times inaccurate, paragraph. It does show a fundamental knowledge of the role of judicial review, but the examples are descriptive and not entirely accurate. The examples have also not been made relevant as the student has assumed that such rulings will necessarily be adhered to. The final sentence is typical of a student eager to show they have addressed the question without providing any real analytical substance.

> The US Supreme Court is better at protecting rights because everyone must obey its rulings. When the Supreme Court passes a case, the government must do what the Supreme Court says, so gay marriage is now legal because of the Supreme Court. In the UK, the government can still ignore the Supreme Court because it is sovereign, not the Court. This means that the US Court can protect people against the government. In the UK, prisoners still do not have the vote despite being told by the courts that they should have. This difference exists because of structural differences in the two countries. In the USA, the Constitution is sovereign whereas in the UK it is Parliament.

e This is a weak and waffly paragraph, which skirts around a brilliant point but is poorly made, and again has some inaccuracies. The point about prisoners voting came from the ECHR not the Supreme Court; however, the theory is still correct. The point is made in a clumsy and repetitive way, however, and lacks the political vocabulary or demonstrated understanding to push into higher levels. The student has made an effort to include comparative theories but has not linked it very well to the point they have made.

> The UK Supreme Court is better at protecting civil rights as it is more independent. In the USA, the government appoints justices, meaning they are biased. In the UK, they are independently appointed, meaning they do not have to listen to the government and are more likely to vote against the government. For example, in a gay rights case, the court found for a gay couple and against the Christian B&B owners who would not let them stay. In the USA, this decision might have been made on the ideology of the justices which can be described as liberal and conservative.

e Again, a waffly paragraph with a reasonable foundation of knowledge but the student is describing what they know rather than ensuring they are answering the question. The example given is valid but does not match the point made as the case was not against the government. Equally, language such as 'bias' is undeveloped and indicates a very basic understanding of the courts.

> Both UK and US Supreme Courts have struggled to protect rights after terrorism. Guantanamo Bay in the USA and the Terrorism Act in the UK have both infringed on civil rights and yet both still exist because the government is stronger than the Supreme Court.

e This very brief paragraph is indicative of a student who has run out of time; timing is crucial and only practice makes perfect. The student makes a valid point and identifies a valid example, but little more.

e **5/12 marks awarded.** This is middle Level 2 answer which shows a reasonable grasp of fundamentals but limited explicit understanding of the question asked. The knowledge is more than superficial (Level 1) but the student does not develop their points to show accuracy or relevance (AO1). This student is regurgitating what they have revised and gains some marks. The answer requires far more analysis, showing why each court could be considered effective and drawing a considered judgement, as well as a much closer focus on the question (AO2) to really succeed.

US democracy and participation

Analyse the similarities between the party systems of the USA and UK.   (12 marks)

In your answer you must consider the relevance of a least one comparative theory.

e These 'analyse' questions require you to apply at least one of the comparative theories to show how the UK and USA are similar or different. In this question you simply need to take a similarity and explain how one of the three comparative theories can explain why that similarity exists. This should be repeated to cover three or four similarities in your answer.

Student answer

Both the USA and UK have strong two-party systems which are supported by the first-past-the-post voting system. **a** **b** FPTP used for Congress, president and Parliament discourages voters from selecting third parties because it is likely to lead to wasted votes. The structural theory is therefore very important in explaining the similarities between the party systems as the voting system creates a structure which strongly influences voting behaviour. In the USA third parties gain virtually no votes with the third-placed candidate, Gary Johnson, libertarian gaining only 3.3% of the vote. Furthermore, even when third parties do gain votes, the structure of the voting system can prevent third parties from gaining seats and power. The Liberal Democrats in the UK receive more votes than third parties in the USA but still gain few seats. In 2015, it was UKIP which was restricted, gaining 3.8m votes but only one seat, allowing two parties to dominate.

e This is a good opening paragraph for the compulsory 12-mark question. **a** It does not write an introduction but takes a strong approach by directly answering the question. **b** It directly answers the question by comparing the two countries in the opening sentence. In addition, the answer follows the command to analyse, which means applying one of the comparative theories. It uses the structural approach to explain how the voting system leads to a similarity in the party systems.

The two-party system has also been encouraged in both countries by their dominance in campaign expenditure. Again, it is the structural theory which can be applied to explain the similarities in the party system because their access to money is a structure which limits smaller parties. The two main parties have been able to attract greater funding, arguably helping them to run more effective campaigns and maintain their grip on power. In the UK, apart from the 2010 coalition government, all governments have been either Labour or Conservative and the two main parties typically gain over 85% of seats and in the US Congress the two main parties are close to 100% dominant. These main parties massively outspend their rivals. In 2015 Conservatives spent £15.6m compared to the Liberal Democrats' £3.7m. In the USA the contrast is even stronger. The rational theory could also be used to explain donations. **c** Pressure groups and individuals are more likely to give money to the two main parties because they perceive they have the most chance of winning. For a business leader, it is rational to give money to a possible winner rather than a likely loser who will have no power after the election. This is perhaps why the main parties in both countries attract most funding.

e This paragraph can be highly rewarded. **c** It makes use of two different theories, adding the rational theory. This is not essential — your answer only needs to apply one of the theories but it provides a useful contrast and shows good understanding, which will be rewarded.

In both **d** countries there is evidence of multi-party politics with third parties exercising some influence, especially in some regions. Voters are able to act as rational actors by voting for whatever they believe is the best party or candidate for them. This has led to some success for third parties in both **d** countries. This is more **d** noticeable in the UK, where devolution has allowed third parties such as the SNP and Plaid Cymru to gain significant power. In the USA third parties have sometime performed well on a national level. Even when they have not won elections they have often been able to influence the policy of the two main parties. The rise of the Reform Party in the 1990s strongly influenced the Democrats and Republicans to adopt some of its key policies to restrict its popularity. While Ross Perot did not win in 1992 or 1996, one of his main policies, a balanced budget, was adopted by the big two. Rational voting for third parties has therefore allowed them to have some success in both countries.

e This paragraph maintains focus on the question by exploring another similarity and linking it to a comparative theory. **d** Notice how often comparative words or phrases are used

e **12/12 marks awarded.** This is a very strong answer, which gets to the top of Level 4. It shows accurate knowledge and understanding of similarities between the party systems in each country and a good range of contemporary evidence from both countries (AO1). It also consistently applies comparative theories in order to explain the similarities (AO2). In each paragraph, the student follows a useful format, comparing the two countries, applying a comparative theory and giving (comparative) evidence.

◼ Section C questions

Note: Section C questions will be asked on *entirely* United States topics.

Question 1

Evaluate the significance of midterm elections. (30 marks)

ⓔ The significance of midterms can be evaluated by looking at how specific midterm elections change the way in which politics operates, such as the impact on the power of the president or the effectiveness of Congress. This question focuses specifically on midterms (those elections in the middle of a president's term) and not elections for president or congressional elections which take place at the same time as the presidential election.

Student answer

Midterm elections are significant because they offer citizens an opportunity to vote for Congress in the middle of a president's term in office. This adds democratic value to the US voting system with elections being held at frequent intervals. In addition, the significance of midterms can be judged by their impact. Midterm elections can have a major bearing on the power of political parties (through control of Congress), the power of the incumbent president and the policy direction of the country. On the other hand their significance may not be particularly high when they lead to little or no change in these areas. Some midterms may simply maintain the status quo.

ⓔ This is a good introduction for a 30-mark essay. It demonstrates a focus on the topic (of midterms) and a clear understanding of the key word 'significance', showing how the answer will evaluate that significance, by examining the impact of midterms in different ways. This also serves to give an outline of the key points covered in the answer.

Midterms are highly significant because they can lead to a major decline in presidential power ⓐ. This occurs when the president's party goes from majority to minority control in one or more chambers. This leaves the president facing a hostile majority which is more likely to scrutinise presidential actions and oppose his policies. President Obama faced a major loss of power in the 2010 midterms when the Democrats lost control of the House. Congressional Republicans then opposed his policies as well as using committees to investigate the executive branch. Midterms are highly significant because they can lead to a major decline in presidential power ⓐ. This occurs when the president's party goes from majority to minority control in one or more chambers. This leaves the president facing a hostile majority which is more likely to scrutinise presidential actions and oppose his policies. President Obama faced a major loss of power in the 2010 midterms when the Democrats lost control of the House. Congressional Republicans then opposed his policies as well as using committees to investigate the executive branch. Having achieved legislative success with the Affordable

---

Care Act and the American Recovery and Reinvestment Act (a $787 billion economic stimulus package disliked by fiscally conservative Republicans) in his first 2 years, he faced major opposition to his agenda after that, with Congress rejecting comprehensive immigration reform and greater gun control. With the president's party typically losing seats in Congress it is common for midterms to have a negative impact on presidential power. President Clinton (1994) and President George W. Bush (2006) both experienced similar fates, losing a congressional majority and much of their power. **b**

e This is a strong paragraph. **a** After a direct answer to the question in the first sentence it judges the extent of significance, for example by using words such as 'highly'. **b** As well as giving good detail and range of evidence, it makes a judgement about the Obama evidence by saying how typical this example is. Showing that the Obama example is commonplace helps to demonstrate the extent to which midterms are significant.

Midterms do not always lead to this kind of change, however. In some cases they have minimal impact on presidential power because they do not lead to a change in party control. This means that the president does not lose (or gain) significant levels of power. In 1998, President Clinton, having faced divided government for 4 years, saw this continue after congressional elections. In this sense, the 1994 elections were more significant in bringing about change than those of 1998. The 2002 midterms were highly significant in a different way from most midterms because they allowed the president to increase his power levels. **c** As a result of the events of 9/11, George Bush and the Republicans (the GOP) extended their majority in both chambers. This midterm led to one of the most powerful presidencies in the history of the USA in which Congress was arguably highly subservient in allowing an extension of federal government power (such as the Patriot Act, extending the power of the security agencies with major concerns about civil liberties) and controversial policies, such as the initiation of the Iraq War. Some midterms will therefore be more important than others, although many are significant in reducing presidential power. **d**

e This is another strong paragraph, which evaluates the extent of significance by showing how some midterms may have limited impact. **c** The comparisons between different midterms provide clear analysis. **d** The final sentence provides more evaluation, making a judgement about the extent of significance based on the first two main paragraphs.

Midterms are also significant because they can lead to a change in the policy direction of the country. If a party loses control of one or more chambers then the new majority party can set an alternative political agenda. Midterms are increasingly nationalised with senior party leaders developing a US-wide agenda which voters can identify with. This can help to give a mandate to those party leaders and the national party platform. **e** Incoming speakers, with a more recent mandate than the president, can assert a degree of control. Both President

Obama (after the 2010 midterms) and President Bush (after the 2006 midterms) were forced to accept the alternative agendas of Speaker Boehner and Speaker Pelosi to a great extent. In 2006 Pelosi's 100-hour agenda was largely accepted by the president with a more liberal agenda which included an increase in the federal minimum wage and the removal of federal subsidies for major oil companies. f

e This paragraph achieves marks in all three assessment objectives, with a direct answer to the question. **e** There is some analysis (AO2), which could perhaps be developed a little when it hints that midterms have become *more* significant over time. **f** While it provides good evidence, it could have made even more judgement about the evidence, as the student has done in previous paragraphs.

On the other hand, the extent of policy change can be limited. In some cases the president may resort to imperial presidency powers in order to bypass Congress and achieve policy goals. Divided government does not therefore lead to a change of policy direction. Obama used executive orders to achieve immigration reform and gun control after the GOP-led Congress refused to pass legislation in these areas. In addition, rather than leading to a change in policy direction, the result may lead to gridlock in which little gets done. This was the case after the 2010 midterms in which Obama and Congress failed to agree on a series of policies including the budget, defence and immigration. Congress became the least productive ever, passing fewer bills than in any other period. This is highly significant because it has a major negative impact on the functioning of government. g

e This paragraph provides a useful assessment of the argument in the previous paragraph. There is some good evaluation (AO3), as well as lots of AO1 knowledge. **g** The final sentence provides particularly strong evaluation when it shows an understanding of different ways in which midterms can be significant and judges the extent.

Different midterms will be significant in different ways. While many focus on policy direction and impact on the power of the president, others have more unusual importance. The 1998 midterms were unusual because of their personal nature connected to the possible removal of President Clinton from office. The GOP, under the speakership of Newt Gingrich, focused almost entirely on the Lewinsky Affair. The impact of relative Democrat success in these elections was to end the attempt to remove Clinton from the presidency, with the public restricting the GOP majority and effectively presenting a view that they wanted an end to the feud over this particular issue. This midterm was perhaps less significant than it would have been had the GOP extended its congressional majority. On the other hand, it was highly significant because it helped prevent the president from being removed from office.

e This paragraph is particularly strong for its evaluation of the extent of significance by showing how some midterms will have a particular significance which others do not. It shows that the 1998 midterms were significant and makes a judgement about the extent of this.

Midterms are always significant in terms of their impact. Many midterms are extremely important because they affect the power levels of the president and the policy direction of the country. It is clear that some have greater impact than others. This occurs particularly when there is a change in party majority, usually leading to a major decrease in presidential power. Other midterms are significant for specific reasons such as the 1998 midterm and the fate of President Clinton.

ⓔ This is a good approach to a conclusion, giving a definite answer to a question. Conclusions should not simply state that there are arguments on both sides but come to a clear judgement based on the main arguments and evidence presented in the essay.

ⓔ 26/30 marks awarded. This is a very strong answer, which matches the Level 5 descriptor. It shows thorough and in-depth knowledge and understanding of the process of midterms, including in-depth use of evidence (AO1). It also has perceptive analysis (rather than merely consistent analysis — Level 4) of the different ways in which midterms can be significant and the factors which affect that significance (AO2). It also constructs fully relevant evaluation of the importance of midterms with fully substantiated arguments (or perhaps mostly effective arguments) with a fully focused and justified conclusion (AO3). It uses a typical essay structure, in which it presents a series of paired arguments and counter-arguments as well as making judgements about the relative strengths of each pair.

Question 2

Evaluate whether judicial activism can be justified in a democracy.   (30 marks)

ⓔ This question requires a good understanding not only of judicial activism, but also of 'democracy'. The question is not focusing on the merits or otherwise of judicial activism, but on how it relates and works in a democracy. For top marks you should be thinking about different kinds of democracy (representative, liberal, pluralist etc.). You need to review the factors that show why judicial activism both can and cannot be justified, but your essay should have an overall argument, not merely describing the whole way through.

Student answer

Judicial activism is a theory of judicial action which suggests that justices should use their position to promote desirable social ends. In a democracy, judicial activism is a cause of debate as judges are unelected and therefore in acting like this they seem to be making law without a mandate, such as in the recent gay marriage case. **ⓐ** However, without judicial activism, there is a chance that minority views and rights could be ignored by an elected government interested only in votes. **ⓑ** Ultimately, it depends on the type of democracy in question as to whether judicial action can be seen as justified **ⓒ**.

e This is a solid introduction, which follows a good basic structure — the 3D's — define, discuss, direction. *a* Define the terms of the question. *b* Discuss: show what the argument is about. *c* Direction: what are you likely to argue, with a hint of why. This is a good way of ensuring your introduction is relevant rather than simply waffling in the direction of the essay title and hoping for some marks.

> Judicial activism is justified in a liberal democracy where a high priority is placed on the protection of rights. Elected branches of government such as the president and Congress may be more interested in winning votes and therefore willing to infringe on minority rights if it gains them popularity. The opening of Guantanamo Bay may be seen as a way to protect the majority, yet detaining terror suspects without trial is not in line with a liberal democracy. It is therefore most likely justices who are able to protect these individuals because they are unelected and therefore do not have to be concerned with public opinion and so they can defend their constitutional rights, which the government might not.

e This is a solid first paragraph with accurate knowledge. The theory is strong, showing good understanding of types of democracy. However, the whole paragraph is theoretical. It would be good to have an example to underpin this, such as *Hamdan* v *Rumsfeld* (2006). The analysis of why judicial activism can be justified is clear, if theoretical.

> However, such actions are more controversial when considering America as a representative democracy. The elected branches of government have a mandate from the people and therefore if they choose to enact policies such as Guantanamo Bay it is on the behalf of their constituents. The judges, by contrast, are unelected and therefore unaccountable. In a representative democracy this effectively means that they can act in a way that might be 'tyrannous' without having to worry about losing their job. When 26 states sued the national government to prevent the enforcement of Obamacare, the Supreme Court ruled to keep the law even though a majority of states were against it. Such action could be seen to undermine the will of the people as expressed through elections and therefore be undemocratic.

e This builds on the paragraph above, showing a balanced argument, which is good. It is a shame that the example jumps from Guantanamo Bay to Obamacare as this somewhat breaks the logic of the argument. Instead, a point could have been made about the protection of minorities at the expense of majorities and Obamacare could have been a separate point — do think about the flow of your essay. Nonetheless, the student does keep trying to answer the question at the end of each paragraph.

> This is particularly notable given how few people are on the Supreme Court in the USA. Just nine judges can have the effect of making new law, which is even more concerning when a ruling is 5–4. Judicial activism suggests that justices should look for cases in which they can promote desirable social outcomes; however, what is a desirable social outcome? To decide this, a justice must apply

some level of ideology to the cases in front of them, usually conservative or liberal. In the case of *Citizens United* v *FEC* (2010), the Court could have chosen not to hear the case as it does get over 8,000 a year. Especially as the Supreme Court had already heard a similar case in 2003 and decided that money did not amount to free speech in an election. However, since 2003, the Court had become more conservative and in taking the case the Court was able to ensure a more conservative outcome — that money was free speech, by 5–4. With just five justices effectively changing national policy, this can be seen as undemocratic.

e It is always advisable to avoid rhetorical questions — your job as a student is to show you have a well thought through answer, not pose more questions! This paragraph is more tenuous than the others. The information is valid yet there is no clear link to judicial activism. It is important to ensure that your paragraphs remain closely tied to the question and using words from the question will help you do this.

Within American democracy, however, if the Supreme Court does not act with judicial activism, it is possible that the elected branches at national or state level could breach the Constitution and yet not be held accountable for it — this itself is tyrannous. The US democracy works on the principle of separation of powers to prevent this, so if the Court chooses to act only in limited circumstances it undermines the entire principle of American constitutional democracy. Obama failed to achieve immigration reform through Congress and therefore acted using executive orders to achieve some reform. However, executive orders are not meant to be a way to get around Congress and they certainly are not meant to be 'law'. If the Supreme Court has acted with 'restraint', deferring to the elected branch, then the president would have been allowed to act in this perhaps unconstitutional manner. Instead, the Court struck down these actions in *US* v *Texas* (2016) which upheld the checks and balances in the Constitution and showed US democracy to work as the Founding Fathers intended.

e This is a much stronger paragraph, which continues to link judicial activism and democracy with a well-explained example which is embedded within the paragraph. It is notable that the AO2 analysis is more than simply a tacked-on sentence at the end but instead makes up at least the final third of the paragraph. This student has now got into the swing of the essay!

Nonetheless, with the Court being willing to decide upon cases of political importance, this perhaps breaches separation of powers. For example, in 2000, the Supreme Court effectively chose the president in deciding the case of *Bush* v *Gore*. In a country of 300 million people, nine justices deciding an election could be argued to be highly undemocratic.

e The shortness of this paragraph suggests a student running out of time. However, it is also a bit repetitive, so it may be that they are running out of things to say. Planning time before you start is never wasted and will help you plan your time and the logic of your essay.

> Overall, judicial activism seems to be a necessity in order to ensure the smooth functioning of US democracy more generally, despite the fact that this means sometimes justices themselves may be seen to undermine representative democracy. However, it is clear that the Founding Fathers placed a good deal of importance on rights through the passage of the Bill of Rights, and to ensure this is upheld, the Supreme Court and judicial activism are necessary and therefore justified.

🄔 This is a reasonably good conclusion that avoids simply repeating the question and does attempt to answer it. It does not really explain why the student reached this conclusion as opposed to the opposite but it does show signs of analytical thought.

🄔 **20/30 marks awarded.** This is a solid essay, which manages to achieve Level 4. The student is clearly attempting to answer the question set, rather than simply write down everything they know, which ensures mostly relevant knowledge (AO1) and a consistent analytical theme throughout (AO2). It needs slightly more thought in terms of the overall flow to make a fully effective argument and is a touch on the short side (AO3). It is important that examples are included but also that they are used rather than simply described, to ensure coherent analysis is constructed — i.e. why have you written about this example (AO2)?

Question 3

Evaluate the view that the US Constitution is now out of date.　　　　(30 marks)

🄔 This question has a key word that many students miss — 'now'. The inclusion of the word 'now' suggests that perhaps something has changed in recent history that means that this debate is more relevant now than it has been before. Do not simply describe factors for and against, instead focus on linking them to recent events — for example, that in two presidential elections since 2000 the 'losing' candidate has won.

Student answer

> The US Constitution was written at the Philadelphia Convention in 1787 by the Founding Fathers. It lays out the power of each branch of government, president, Congress and Supreme Court, as well as how it can be amended. Because the Constitution is written down, some people think it is out of date. However, the Constitution does still work so it might be up to date.

🄔 This is a very descriptive introduction and gains few marks. While it shows knowledge of the Constitution, the point of your exam is not simply to show that you have learnt 'stuff'. You also need to demonstrate that you have developed skills such as evaluation and analysis. This student does not show that they understand the question.

> One reason that the Constitution might be out of date is because of the 2nd Amendment. The 2nd Amendment allows for the 'right to bear arms'; this means that Americans can own guns. While there are some restrictions on what types of gun can be owned, there are more registered guns in America than there are

people. Despite attempts to pass gun control laws, there has been little success because of the Constitution and this has meant that incidents such as the Sandy Hook shooting have happened. It is not likely that the Founding Fathers could imagine machine guns when they wrote this amendment, therefore allowing all Americans guns shows the Constitution to be out of date.

e The knowledge here is sound, if not fully explained and sometimes clumsily expressed. For this type of question, analysis and evaluation are crucial so this student would do better to explain the reasons that the Constitution prevents gun control laws — i.e. a discussion about sovereignty. Equally, 'out of date' suggests that something has changed — there is a fleeting reference to machines guns but development of this would explain the point in far greater depth.

Another reason that the Constitution is out of date is because of the Electoral College. This allows for the winner of an election to actually be the loser. Both George Bush and Donald Trump lost the popular vote yet became the president because they won more Electoral College votes. The Electoral College is therefore undemocratic and in a modern democracy such as America it is out of place. Replacing it would allow for representative democracy to work more effectively. Linked to this, the electoral process in the Constitution also gives every state the same power in the Senate. This was ok when there were 13 states that were not so different in size, but today huge states like California and Texas have the same number of senators as Wyoming or Alaska. This seems very undemocratic and suggests that the Constitution needs to be reformed.

e There are a number of valid points here with some links drawn but all too briefly made, lacking developed examples or analysis. It is also beginning to look a little more like a list of arguments rather than one coherent essay. You should be aiming to persuade your examiner, not write them a list of arguments to choose from.

The Bill of Rights is also out of date because the world has changed so much since the Founding Fathers wrote the Constitution. For example, rights like gay marriage and abortion are not protected in the Constitution, or even the right to privacy. Because of this, it is possible for a government to try and take away these rights. Texas tried to make it more difficult to get an abortion in that state in 2016 and it was only the Supreme Court ruling that stopped this. These rights should be protected better in the modern world.

e This is a valid point that perhaps could be linked to the first paragraph about the 2nd Amendment to make a stronger, more coherent argument. There is *no need* to say 'for example' — your examiner will know it's an example by what you write after that! The example is relevant but brief and the whole paragraph very descriptive.

On the other hand, the Constitution is not out of date because the Supreme Court is able to interpret it to keep it up to date. The Founding Fathers might not have known about Guantanamo Bay a, but the Bill of Rights has helped protect the detainees there because the Supreme Court has ruled they should have access to civilian courts. By interpreting the Constitution the Supreme Court keeps it up to date, for example making rulings on abortion and gay marriage. If a new constitution were written it would suffer from the same arguments about being dated so this way it can be kept relevant.

e The quality of writing is important when making an argument — statements like **a** are redundant as of course the Founding Fathers wouldn't have known! The student is repeating a standard paragraph formula at this point — identify a point, identify an example, try and link it to the question. There is too little analysis or evaluation.

Also, the Constitution is not out of date as it still works. While the original USA was only 13 states, there are now 50 and each state has its own laws. This means that things like marijuana laws and abortion rights are different in each state. The Founding Fathers wanted to ensure federalism and the Constitution still does, therefore it is not out of date.

e Such a short paragraph is unlikely to have, and in this case doesn't have, much analysis. It relies on knowledge, which is not fully developed, and lacks considered analysis or judgement.

Lastly the Constitution is not out of date because it has been amended. There have been 27 amendments to the Constitution which have been added since it was first written. These have abolished slavery, made an elected Senate and allowed women to vote. By having an amendment process the Constitution has been able to keep up to date.

e This final paragraph rounds off what has become a balanced but ultimately not persuasive, bland list of arguments. This shows knowledge and an understanding of the question but not engagement with it.

There are arguments for and against the Constitution being out of date. It seems that if the Constitution works, and the Supreme Court can continue to update it, then there is no immediate pressure to reform it, therefore it is not out of date.

e This is a weaker conclusion and the judgement drawn is not apparent from the rest of the essay. It also does not fully address the question, which is not about reform but whether the Constitution is out of date — be wary of rewriting the question.

e **15/30 marks awarded.** Overall, this is a mid-Level 3 essay relying on AO1 knowledge rather than engaging in persuasive writing. It demonstrates accurate knowledge but weaker understanding and therefore sits in the middle level of AO1. You must remember that you are not simply trying to show the examiner you have learnt 'stuff'; you are showing off your skills and ability to interpret and answer the question set. The analysis is logical but bland and basic; it shows logical reasoning but needs development and consistency to gain more marks (AO2). Writing an essay as a list of arguments, especially in two halves like this, is not advisable as while there are conclusions, they are not all justified (AO3).

Knowledge check answers

1 This clause allows Congress to make any law needed in order to carry out its powers; this allows Congress to 'stretch' its power beyond the powers laid out in the Constitution.

2 From the case of *Marbury* v *Madison* (1803) (to strike down federal law) and *Fletcher* v *Peck* (1810)

3 The delegates at the Philadelphia Convention of 1787 at which the US Constitution was drawn up

4 Baron de Montesquieu, from his book *De l'esprit des lois* (The Spirit of the Laws)

5 By including the Electoral College and an unelected Senate, which could counteract the public vote

6 10th Amendment. Other rights are protected throughout, e.g. Article I guarantees control elections.

7 It allows it to declare law (federal and state) unconstitutional and therefore null and void.

8 A clause in Article I that allows Congress control over interstate (and foreign) trade

9 A trustee acts using their conscience in the best interests of their constituents; a delegate must act as directed by their constituents.

10 Midterm elections involve elections to Congress. They are *only* those elections which take place in the middle of the president's term, occurring every 4 years. 'Congressional elections' covers *all* congressional elections including midterms.

11 Impeachment is an exclusive power of the House and determines if there are sufficient grounds to believe that a public official has committed a serious crime. It does not involve removal from office. The Senate alone decides whether or not to remove someone from office.

12 The person already holding a particular political office

13 Yes. It can refer to any group in Congress, such as the Freedom or Democratic Caucus. It can also refer to an election process in primary voting.

14 There are several obstacles, such as the need for House and Senate agreement, the presidential veto, the power of congressional committees, divided government, and low levels of party unity.

15 In several ways, such as congressional committees, votes on presidential proposals, ratifying treaties, ratifying appointments, impeachment.

16 The separation of powers and checks and balances give 18 enumerated powers to Congress, which allows it power over the president such as the veto override and budget control.

17 The main idea is that the separation of powers helps prevent the executive from dominating Congress, whereas in the UK the government dominates Parliament through its majority and the whip system.

18 Powers which are not written into the Constitution but are taken anyway

19 The Army and the Navy; the Air Force did not exist at the time the Constitution was written.

20 The two most obvious examples are 9/11 and Hurricane Katrina in 2005, both G. W. Bush.

21 They won by winning more Electoral College votes.

22 All executive power is vested in a single president.

23 EXOP has no constitutional power.

24 In their final 2 years in office

25 Arthur J. Schlesinger wrote *The Imperial Presidency*, looking mainly at Nixon and the significant power he had amassed, including over the Vietnam War.

26 In the State of the Union address to Congress

27 The USA was still surrounded by imperial European powers (Britain, France and Spain) and they probably expected the need for the president to act to protect the newly formed United States of America.

28 They interpret the Constitution; its ruling can only be changed by changing the Constitution itself.

29 54–45

30 Scalia was a conservative and Garland was a centrist, therefore not a like-for-like replacement.

31 Trump may get to replace more justices during his tenure.

32 Freedoms of speech, religion, press, association and petition for redress of grievance

33 'Friends of the Court'

34 The principle of 'letting the decision stand', referring to previous Supreme Court decisions

35 There is no upper age limit

36 The presidential nomination process does *not* elect the president to the White House. It refers to primary and caucus elections, in which parties choose their presidential candidate.

37 Primary voting uses traditional voting methods with a ballot paper. Caucus voting requires voters to attend a meeting and vote publicly.

38 A swing state is any state that might switch control from one party to another. This could include presidential or Senate elections. It is the opposite of a safe state.

39 1 = A; 2 = A and B; 3 = C; 4 = B and arguably A

40 Social and moral policy, including crime, national economy and social welfare

41 An access point is any powerful political organisation which an interest group can effectively influence.

42 PACs: are organisations set up by an interest group or business so that it can donate money during elections, subject to campaign finance restrictions. SuperPACs: usually created to influence elections through advertising rather than donating. There are no restrictions on donations to SuperPACS or the amount of money they spend.

43 Federal Election Campaign Act (FECA) and Bipartisan Campaign Reform Act (BCRA) in the USA; and The Political Parties, Elections and Referendums Act 2000 (PPERA) in the UK

Index

Index